Interpreting Prophetic Literature

Interpreting Prophetic Literature

Historical and Exegetical Tools for Reading the Prophets

James D. Nogalski

WESTMINSTER
JOHN KNOX PRESS
LOUISVILLE · KENTUCKY

First edition
Published by Westminster John Knox Press
Louisville, Kentucky

15 16 17 18 19 20 21 22 23 24—10 9 8 7 6 5 4 3 2 1

Book design by Drew Stevens
Cover design by Allison Taylor

Library of Congress Cataloging-in-Publication Data

Nogalski, James.
  Interpreting prophetic literature : historical and exegetical tools for reading the prophets / James D. Nogalski. — First edition.
        pages cm
  Includes index.
  ISBN 978-0-664-26120-7 (alk. paper)
  1. Bible. Prophets—Hermeneutics.   2. Bible. Prophets—Theology.   I. Title.
  BS1505.52.N64   2015
  224'.06—dc23

                                                             2015009066

Most Westminster John Knox Press books are available at special quantity discounts when purchased in bulk by corporations, organizations, and special-interest groups. For more information, please e-mail SpecialSales@wjkbooks.com.

To my students, past and future,
whose questions have inspired me

Contents

Abbreviations

2fs	Second feminine singular
2ms	Second masculine singular
2mp	Second masculine plural
3fs	Third feminine singular
CEB	Common English Bible
COS	*Context of Scripture*, ed. W.W. Hallo, 3 vols. (Leiden: Brill, 2003)
ESV	English Standard Version
JPS	Jewish Publication Society
KJV	King James Version
LXX	Septuagint (the Greek Old Testament)
LXX (Brenton)	*The Septuagint with Apocrypha: Greek and English*. Lancelot C. L. Brenton (Peabody: Hendrickson, 1987).
MT	Masoretic Text (the Hebrew Bible)
NASB	*New American Standard Bible*
NET	New English Translation
NICOT	New International Commentary on the Old Testament
NIV	*New International Version*
NKJV	*New King James Version*
NLT	*New Living Translation*
NRSV	New Revised Standard Version

1

Getting Started

The majority of this book will focus upon reading the literature of the Latter Prophets (Isaiah, Jeremiah, Ezekiel, and the Twelve), not to create experts in the individual books, but to introduce students to the process of understanding and interpreting prophetic literature. In introductions to the Old Testament as a whole or to the prophetic writings in particular, the art of learning to read this literature is seldom given the attention most beginning students need. Further, textbooks dealing with the exegetical process often suffer from two deficits faced by beginning students approaching prophetic literature. First, most introductions to the exegetical process assume that the student has some measure of competence in Hebrew. In both seminaries and colleges, however, most students have their first exposure to prophetic literature before they have completed a Hebrew course. Second, without exception, introductions to exegetical methodology illustrate the various methods from narrative literature (i.e., the Torah and the Former Prophets [Joshua, Judges, 1 and 2 Samuel, and 1 and 2 Kings]). Seldom are prophetic speeches, forms, or collections given any attention at all. As a result of these two shortcomings, beginning students struggle to understand the poetry and the rhetorical logic of smaller and larger units within the prophetic writings.

Interpreting Prophetic Literature seeks to fill this gap for beginning students. It will focus upon the art of reading prophetic literature without assuming students are working from the Hebrew text. It will focus upon illustrating the markers and the methods most important for understanding prophetic literature. It will get students started in the process of reading these texts. Examples provided will be illustrative, not comprehensive.

What this book will not do is to replace the use of a traditional textbook that introduces each prophet and each prophetic book. This book does not attempt to serve as an introduction to the prophetic writings. It will not deal extensively with the historical backgrounds of the individual prophetic books. Rather, this book will attempt to supplement such introductions by focusing upon the art of reading prophetic literature.

Before turning to the interpretive process in chapters 2–4, this chapter will do two things. First, it will offer a few comments about the broader ancient Near Eastern background of prophets and prophecy, as well as the role of prophets in the narrative literature of the Hebrew Bible. Second, this chapter will provide an overview of the interpretive process itself, including some suggestions for students on how to use multiple English translations as a means of compensating for the lack of access to Hebrew.

PROPHECY, PROPHETS, AND PROPHETIC BOOKS

In order to understand and to appreciate Old Testament prophetic literature as it has been transmitted to us, one must realize that prophecy has a long history in the ancient Near East. Prophets can be documented in the region more than half a millennium prior to the earliest known reference to the nation of Israel. Prophets also appear in Old Testament narratives that recount episodes from the story of Israel and Judah long before the time of the prophetic figures for whom the collections within the Latter Prophets are named. Yet these narrative traditions regarding prophets do not adequately prepare modern readers to understand and to engage the Latter Prophets. The four scrolls that comprise the Latter Prophets (Isaiah, Jeremiah, Ezekiel, and the Twelve) are composite collections containing speeches, commentary, narratives, and various poetic forms. The arrangement of the material within these scrolls demonstrates that sources from different time periods have been transmitted, periodically structured, and updated with newer material that reflects changing realities. These three issues (transmission, shaping, and updating) will be discussed very briefly to provide some context from which to begin learning to read the prophetic literature of the Hebrew Bible.

Prophecy in the Ancient Near East

Prophecy in the ancient Near East (ANE) has a long history. Already in the eighteenth century BCE prophets played a significant role in the political and religious life of the Mesopotamian community at Mari. The Mari tablets include quite a number of letters and reports concerning prophetic figures. These accounts referred to prophets using a variety of terms, terms whose meaning suggests that the prophets in Mari divided themselves into functional groups according to the type of revelation they practiced. This diversity of practices suggests that in Mari the role of prophets and prophecy had already developed a complex social network and function.

Terms used to refer to these prophetic figures include *āpilu* (meaning roughly, "one who answers," *assinnu* (male cult prostitute, or perhaps a eunuch), the *muḫḫû* (the ecstatic), the *nabû* ("the diviner), and the *barû* (the one who sees [i.e., interprets omens]). The first three of these appear in the Mari texts while the last one appears in Old Babylonian texts. Most of these figures, it is presumed, had some connection to the cult, but most of them we know because they, or their speeches, are referenced in the royal correspondence associated with king Zimri Lim of Mari (1779–1757 BCE). In addition to the variety of names used to refer to those offering advice on behalf of the gods at Mari, one also finds a wide variety of types of divination, including augury, dream interpretation, and oracles. Many of these prophetic figures were required to include pieces of their hair and hems from the garments with their statements. While it is not entirely clear how these items functioned, they imply a serious ritual designed to prove that the prophet should be considered reliable. In fact, it is not uncommon that the *āpilu* include reference to confirmation of the message by some other form of divination (e.g., extispicy, the use of animal entrails to predict the future). This range of terms and implied functions in Mari thus appears to have been even broader than the relationships implied among the biblical prophets.

Reading through this correspondence, one is frequently reminded of a significant difference between these prophetic reports and Old Testament prophetic literature. Often, such documents were recovered as part of some kind of official archive. Consequently, these accounts served a very different function from prophetic literature in that they were either addressed to some particular government official or, in later texts, found at the palace of Assyrian kings. They may contain information intended for the officials conducting the divination.

Consider the examples of sixty-three recorded "Mesopotamian Omens" listed in *COS* 1:423–26. These oracles illustrate a variety of divinatory techniques including observation of animal entrails (extispicy), unusual births, human behavior, random events (cledonomancy), dreams (oneiromancy), and reactions of oil and water when a stone is dropped into a basin (lecanomancy). They record various signs to observe. As such, they serve as a resource for practitioners of these divinatory arts.

See also the list of dream meanings that recount various dream images, followed by an assessment (either "good" or "bad") and an explanation. The top of the columns begins: "If a man sees himself in a dream . . ." What follows contains various examples of dreams and their significance:

"Eating the flesh of a donkey. Good. It means his promotion.
Eating the flesh of a crocodile. Good. [It means] living off the property of
    an official."

"Eating a filleted catfish. Bad. His seizure by a crocodile.
Seeing his face in a mirror. Bad. It means another wife."[1]

Both the collection of oracles and the dream book indicate the formulations were intended as resources for those who were offering these services, not for those who requested them.

Prophets in the Old Testament

By contrast, oracles recounted in biblical prophecy are largely directed against the community itself. Often, even when oracles are directed against an individual, such as a king or another prophet, those oracles are recounted in ways that make it clear that the story is told for the benefit of the reader. For example, consider Amos 7:10–17. This text contains a brief episode of confrontation between Amos, the prophet, and Amaziah, the (presumably chief) priest at Bethel. It is the voice of the narrator, however, who structures the conversation that provides the biographical information necessary to make sense of this confrontation.

The didactic function of the prophetic corpus should not be overlooked. In point of fact, all four scrolls of the Former Prophets (Joshua, Judges, 1 and 2 Samuel, and 1 and 2 Kings) and of the Latter Prophets (Isaiah, Jeremiah, Ezekiel, and the Twelve) demonstrate that, whatever the sources utilized in compiling these collections, the collections have been shaped with an eye toward their transmission for and reflection by later generations. They do not present themselves as the property of priests or kings, but as words addressed to the people of YHWH.

Prophets serving deities other than YHWH appear in the Old Testament, though usually in polemical contexts where these prophets are being condemned or eliminated. Their presence, however, suggests that biblical writers were aware of prophets working for other deities inside and outside their country. One of the most prominent stories inside the Bible concerns the prophet Balaam in the time of Moses (Num. 22–24). Balaam was a foreign prophet, also known from an inscription outside the Bible (Deir `Alla), although the Deir `Alla text comes from several centuries later than the time in which the exodus story is set.[2] These extrabiblical texts portray Balaam as a very powerful prophetic seer. By contrast, the Balaam stories in Numbers 22–24 recount several ways in which YHWH circumscribes Balaam's power so as to prove the impotence of foreign prophets against YHWH.

Such appropriation of other traditions illustrates one way in which prophetic narratives function within larger stories.

Similarly, prophetic narratives illustrate the power of YHWH over the power of foreign deities in Old Testament narratives. Prophets of Baal are defeated by Elijah in the reign of Ahab (1 Kgs. 18); later, Jehu defeats the prophets of Asherah (2 Kgs. 10:18–31) in the middle of the ninth century BCE. These stories indicate that these prophets of foreign gods were involved in sacrifice, and they even presuppose the presence of a Baal temple. Later, texts indicate that the worship of Baal was still advocated by prophets serving Baal in the late seventh century (Jer. 2:8; cf. Zeph. 1:4–5).

Prophets of YHWH play a major role in Israel and Judah in the Former Prophets (Joshua, Judges, 1 and 2 Samuel, 1 and 2 Kings). To put this role in perspective, one need only contemplate the implications of the way one speaks about the Old Testament canon. In Christian tradition, the second major section of the canon has often been called the historical books. By contrast, in the Hebrew Bible (the Tanak), the second section of the canon is called the Prophets (Nebiim). Remarkably, though, the first four scrolls of the Nebiim in the Hebrew Bible (Joshua, Judges, 1 and 2 Samuel, and 1 and 2 Kings) constitute the same books that form the foundation of "the historical books" of the Christian canon.

What a difference names can make! Each of these names focuses upon a significant aspect of these narrative texts. One can understand how these books came to be called historical books in the Christian canon: they tell the story of Israel and Judah from the Hebrews' entry into the land until Jerusalem's destruction. It is not a history in the modern sense, but a theologically shaped recounting of that story. However, calling these writings the historical books also underplays the role that prophets play in the story itself. In fact, beginning in Deuteronomy 18, the role of Moses as prophet prepares the ground for the ongoing role of prophetic leadership when entering the land, beginning in Joshua.

In Deuteronomy 18 Moses is presented as the prophet par excellence. A significant criterion concerning the role of the prophet is the juxtaposition of commands prohibiting divination, as practiced by the nations, in 18:9–14 with the promise from YHWH in 18:15–22 (see especially 18:15, 18) that YHWH will provide Israel with prophets like Moses when they enter the land. The primary role of prophets in Deuteronomy 18:18 is to speak faithfully the words that YHWH has communicated to them. One certainly sees this role of prophet play out in many of the episodes in the Former Prophets, but that is not the only way in which prophets appear within the larger narrative. In the Former Prophets, one finds prophets performing duties as ecstatics, disciples, counselors, insurgents, and intermediaries for YHWH.

Bands of (ecstatic) prophets can be seen in passages like 1 Samuel 10. Periodically, these groups appear in narrative texts, and the groups are portrayed as ecstatic prophets operating on the margins of society, especially in narratives concerning the early monarchic period in the books of Samuel and Kings. In 1 Samuel 10, for example, Saul joins a band of ecstatic prophets and becomes the object of ridicule (1 Sam. 10:10–12).

Elisha's disciples in Bethel would be another such group, and one also sees a certain kind of institutionalizing in this narrative. Groups of prophets could band together formally, as 2 Kings 2 suggests. There a group of prophets are called "sons of prophets," and they recognize Elijah as their leader. The term "prophet," then, applies both to the disciples and to the leader. At Elijah's death, these disciples transferred their allegiance to Elisha (2 Kgs. 2:15). Many scholars believe that prophetic groups like these may have continued for generations and constituted the groups who transmitted the words of prophets after their death. Some call these groups schools, while others refer to them as tradents, a more neutral term that may originally have included followers of a prophet (before they were transmitted by other groups of scribes and temple officials).

The fact that these groups were known as "sons of prophets" suggests that the prophet would have been known as the "father" of the group. This idea helps one to understand the mocking tone of the proverb associated with Saul in 1 Samuel 10:11–12, where an unnamed character is quoted as asking about the relationship of Saul to this group, "And who is their father?" The sarcastic implications seem clear enough. Saul has just been anointed king by Samuel, and Saul becomes one of the prophetic followers. Such language may also lie behind the famous quote of Amos when Amaziah accuses him of prophesying for money. Amos responds, "I am not a prophet nor the son of a prophet" (Amos 7:14). Narrative episodes such as these suggest that while such groups were known in Judah and Israel, they were treated often with suspicion by the political and religious establishment.

Prophets are, however, also depicted in roles of power as political and military counselors. Nathan is presented as a faithful prophet who advised (2 Sam. 7) and then confronted David (2 Sam. 12) before colluding with Bathsheba to arrange for Solomon to become king at David's death (1 Kgs. 1). Prophets also offered oracles to kings concerning military plans, not unlike the prophets delivering messages to kings in the Mari letters. Of course, prophesying for the king created pressure for the prophets to deliver messages that the king wanted to hear. For example, 1 Kings 22 recounts how the king of Israel summoned four hundred prophets to deliver oracles on the outcome of the impending battle. The king of Judah, however, wanted to know whether there was still another prophet, apparently suspecting that the unanimity of so many professional prophets meant they were telling the king what he wanted to hear. These examples of prophets demonstrate that some were deemed reliable and respectable counselors while others were not.

At the same time, prophets could be perceived by political and religious leaders as antagonists, because they dared to speak messages that challenged the king or the king's policy. For example, 2 Kings 9:1–7 demonstrates that Elisha sided with Jehu when Jehu led an insurrection against the house of Ahab. Jehu had his own reasons for revolting, but Elisha threw his support behind Jehu, because Ahab's wife, Jezebel, had been persecuting and killing prophets (2 Kgs. 9:7). To be sure, the biblical text casts the message of the prophets in religious terms, but because this message was directed against the king and the king's family, these actions also had political implications.

Genuine prophets, at their core, are treated as spokespersons for YHWH. Their history of standing against the power structures of what they perceived to be unjust political leaders becomes embedded in the traditions about prophets, even to the point that YHWH's decision to destroy Israel includes the accusation that both Israel and Judah failed to listen to YHWH's prophets: "Yet the Lord warned Israel and Judah by every prophet and every seer, saying, 'Turn from your evil ways and keep my commandments and my statutes, in accordance with all the law that I commanded your ancestors and that I sent to you by my servants the prophets'" (2 Kgs. 17:13). When one sees these dynamics frequently running through the narrative episodes of the story of Judah and Israel, one begins to understand why in Jewish tradition this part of the canon is called the Former Prophets, not the historical books.

Prophetic Books

As noted above, prophets and prophecy play a significant role in the narrative traditions that recount the story of Israel and Judah. Conversely, of the fifteen prophetic figures for whom collections are named within the four scrolls of the Latter Prophets, only two (Isaiah and Jonah) are mentioned by name in the books of 1 and 2 Kings, the primary narrative recounting the story of Israel and Judah. Later narratives of Chronicles and Ezra also refer to three others: Jeremiah (2 Chr. 36:22 = Ezra 1:1), along with Haggai and Zechariah (Ezra 5:1; 6:14). Thus the prophets named in the scrolls of the Latter Prophets play a relatively minor role in the narrative traditions of the Old Testament. These collections have a complex history.

Most models for understanding how prophetic books reached the form in which we now have them do not presume that a prophet simply sat down and composed the book. Rather, most prophetic books developed in stages. The precise nature of these processes differs from one corpus to another, but they share some common patterns. Most (but probably not all) of the prophetic writings began as synopses of prophetic speeches. These speeches were either remembered or transmitted orally by those familiar with the prophet, or they were recorded as brief, written records of memorable sayings.

Over time these sayings were gathered together in small collections where they continued to be studied, interpreted, and applied in new contexts. Sometimes, these new applications were incorporated into the texts, expanding or clarifying the message for later generations. One clear way to see this is by comparing the Hebrew text of Jeremiah with the LXX (Greek text) of the same material. The Hebrew version of Jeremiah is longer than the LXX by roughly one-eighth. Scholars almost universally recognize that the majority of the differences have arisen by relatively late additions to the Hebrew text. The nature of these additions often shows reflection on the text themselves. Consider Jeremiah 6:27–7:4, as shown in chart 1. The additions in the MT version (followed by English translations) show that someone realized that 7:2b–4 represents a new speech, since it is set in the temple (see 7:4), while the previous unit is set outside the city at the crossroads (see 6:16). The second part of 7:2b in the MT further anticipates the change in location by specifying the people of Judah have entered the (temple) gates.

Eventually, these smaller collections were themselves copied together onto scrolls, but in the process these collections were also shaped by those

Chart 1: Hebrew and Greek Versions of Jeremiah 6:27–7:4

English Translation of Jer 6:30–7:4 (MT)	English Translation of Jer 6:27–7:4 (LXX)
[30]They call them rejected silver, because the LORD has rejected them.	[30]Call ye them reprobate silver, because the LORD has rejected them.
[7:1]The word that came to Jeremiah from the LORD, saying, [2]Stand in the gate of the LORD's house and proclaim there this word, and say:	[7:1–2a MISSING IN LXX]
[7:2b]Hear the word of the LORD, all you of Judah, who enter by these gates to worship the LORD!' [3]Thus says the LORD of hosts, the God of Israel, Amend your ways and your deeds, and I will let you dwell in this place, [4]Do not trust in deceptive words, saying, 'This is the temple of the LORD, the temple of the LORD, the temple of the LORD.'	[2]Hear ye the word of the LORD, all Judea. [3]Thus saith the LORD God of Israel, correct your ways and your devices, and I will cause you to dwell in this place. [4]Trust not in yourselves with lying words, for they shall not profit you at all, saying, It is the temple of the LORD, the temple of the LORD.

who combined the collections. For example, consider the collection known as Amos. It has four sections: The oracles against the nations (chaps. 1–2), the sayings (chaps. 3–6), the vision cycle (7:1–9:6), and the increasingly hopeful conclusion (9:7–15). Each of these sections has certain characteristics that distinguish it from the other parts of Amos, but each section has elements that connect it in various ways to the writing as a whole (see chap. 5 in this book). For example, the vision cycle contains five stylized vision reports (7:1–3, 4–6, 7–9; 8:1–3; 9:1–4), but after the third and fourth vision report, one finds other material that is not intrinsically related to the vision reports.

The placement of this nonvisionary material within the vision cycle is not, however, without rationale. The narrative report of the confrontation between Amos and Amaziah in 7:10–17 appears between the third and fourth vision reports because it cites a line from the vision report that precedes it (see reference to Jeroboam dying by the sword in 7:9 and 7:11). Also, 8:4–14 interrupts the fourth (8:1–3) and fifth (9:1–4) vision reports with material that sounds very much like material in the sayings sections and even repeats several key phrases from elsewhere in Amos, so that 8:4–14 functions much like a reprise of some of the key ideas in the book to that point. The fact that the fourth vision announces the "end" of the kingdom and the fifth vision describes the end makes 8:4–14 a logical point to summarize the book to that point. Thus, particularly in some books, the idea of the gradual combination of smaller collections has much to offer with regard to the changing character of the book, but gradual accretion alone is insufficient to explain the development of the book in its entirety.

Periodically, however, some of the scrolls also show signs that they have been shaped, at least in part, thematically or chronologically. For example, Ezekiel lists some fourteen dates in the headings of some of the speeches, and all of them occur in chronological order, except for a couple oracles against Egypt.[3] Nevertheless, Ezekiel shows signs of another common organizing principle in that the majority of statements in chapters 1–24 pronounce words of judgment, while chapters 25–32 contain oracles against foreign nations, and chapters 33–48 largely contain promises.

Ezekiel is not alone in presenting more than one organizing principle. Most of the prophetic writings start with judgment and then move to more hopeful statements. Further, ten of the twelve prophetic writings composing the Book of the Twelve owe their current location to some kind of chronological reflection.[4] Similarly, the scrolls of Isaiah and the Twelve begin with prophets of the eighth century BCE and conclude with prophecies dated to the Persian period (538–332 BCE). Isaiah, however, specifies only one prophet by name, while the Book of the Twelve covers the same time frame with twelve named prophetic figures. Further, each of the twelve writings in the Book of the Twelve shows evidence of its own internal arrangement of prophetic material. For example, Zephaniah follows a pattern similar to Ezekiel, in that Zephaniah begins with judgment sayings (1:1–2:3), moves to a series of oracles against foreign nations that culminates in a surprising pronouncement of judgment against Jerusalem (2:4–3:8), and then concludes with a series of promises (3:9–20).

All of these arrangements suggest that the prophetic writings and scrolls do not constitute a random series of unrelated speeches but have been collected and periodically shaped with an eye toward the larger collection. Consideration of the implications of the shaping of these scrolls represents a relatively recent phenomenon in the scholarly study of prophetic literature, but one that shows considerable promise moving forward. Nevertheless, while these issues are important, they are not the focal point of this book. Introductions to the prophets will describe these elements in greater detail. This book will concentrate on the reading and interpretive process, attempting to guide students who are engaging prophetic texts seriously for the first time. It is to this task that the remainder of this book will now turn.

THE PROCESS OF INTERPRETATION

The idea for this book came from my students. When assigned the task of writing an exposition paper on specific texts, students found it much easier to complete the assignment in the narrative portions of the Old Testament than in prophetic texts. When I consulted introductions to Old Testament interpretive methods, I found they offered no help. These methodologies, almost without exception, illustrate the various methods of Old Testament study with examples from the narrative literature, and perhaps an occasional reference to Psalms. Introductions to prophetic literature are indispensable, but most of these studies focus upon other questions (e.g., date, authorship, and arrangement). As such, they tend to present the fruits of other people's readings of prophetic literature without orienting students to the process of reading prophetic texts closely for themselves.

Introducing the reading process to beginning students, most of whom do not know Hebrew, will thus be the focus of this book. It assumes no knowledge of Hebrew, though occasionally (and unavoidably) it will be necessary to make particular comments about Hebrew words or syntax. These linguistic references, however, are kept to a minimum. Some considerations about how to use English translations *do* need to be explored, and before turning to the more detailed introduction of the interpretive process, a few general remarks about the purpose and process of interpretation may also prove beneficial.

Using English Translations

Using English translations wisely requires students to know something about the nature of the various translations, as well as the purpose for comparing them. The purpose of translation comparison is manifold. Selecting several English translations allows one to compare these translations for help in interpreting phrases, understanding the range of meanings of significant words, noting the presence of variant readings, and analyzing the literary parameters of a text. Make note of places where translations vary from one another in order to assess how significant these variations might be for understanding the text.

There is no such thing as a completely literal translation. All translations involve some level of interpretation on the part of the translator(s). Most translations provide an explanation of the philosophies that guide the translation. These philosophies range from near word-for-word correspondences to dynamic equivalents. Word-for-word translations, such as the NASB, attempt, as far as possible, to provide one English word in the translation for each Hebrew word in the original. Some translations even seek to mirror the sequence of the Hebrew words when translating if it does not contradict English syntactical rules.

More translations use some level of dynamic equivalence, though there is a wide range within this group. Translators using dynamic equivalence prefer to translate by thought units rather than word for word. Some of these translations, such as the NRSV and NIV, attempt to stay fairly close to a word-for-word translation, while others, such as the NLT and CEB, look for ways to translate into more idiomatic speech.

Both ends of the spectrum recognize the need for the translation to read smoothly when read by native English speakers. For this reason, they will often interpret Hebrew phrases into equivalent English phrases, or they will interpret phrases to match more common English syntax. For example, both the NIV and the NRSV will translate the phrase "sons of Israel" as "Israelites" (see, e.g., Gen. 32:32; cf. NASB "sons of Israel"). The NRSV will also translate the phrase as "people of Israel" (see Amos 3:1, where even the KJV translated the phrase as "children of Israel"). These variations occur when the context, in the translation team's opinion, relates to a mixture of men and women. In biblical Hebrew, groups of mixed gender will typically be addressed with masculine terms, while modern English prefers to use gender-neutral terms for groups of men and women.

Interpreters should select several English translations, which will allow one to see the passage through the lens of several different interpreters. This variety provides help in three areas: seeing a word's range of meaning, recognizing variant readings, and determining where prophetic speeches start and stop.

First, English translations may help in determining a range of meanings for significant words. Multiple English words may provide students with a range of meaning for a given Hebrew word. For example, consider Micah 6:8, where the Hebrew word *ḥesed* is translated with a number of different English words in different versions: "He has told you, O mortal, what is good; and what does the LORD require of you but to do justice, and to love *kindness*, and to walk humbly with your God?" The NRSV uses "kindness" to translate *ḥesed*, as do the NIV, ESV, and NASB. Other translations include "mercy" (KJV, NKJ), "goodness" (JPS), and "be faithful" (NET). Each of these translations reflects one aspect of the Hebrew word *ḥesed*, but having to select only one word per translation gives a slightly different slant to this verse in English. Part of the interpreter's job is to decide which nuance makes the best sense of the verse in context.

Second, different words may suggest a variety of word choice or may point to variant readings. For example, consider Zechariah 11:7a, which contains two different types of translation variations. The underlined sections of 11:7a shown in chart 2 illustrate the translation of a verb with roughly synonymous phrases (I became the shepherd/I pastured). By contrast, the italicized portions of the verse represent decisions of the translators regarding the original wording of the verse. The NASB reflects the Hebrew transmission as reflected in the Masoretic Text, which, while complicated syntactically, represents an appositional phrase further delineating "the flock doomed to slaughter." By contrast, translators of the NRSV follow the Greek translation here, which reads "for the Canaanites of the flock" but then interpret "Canaanites" not as an ethnic term but as a slang term meaning "merchants" or "traders"—which it can mean in certain texts.

Despite the very different meanings, the Hebrew behind these two phrases contained the very same consonants. The difference lies in the way the Masoretic Text divides these consonants into two words (*lākēn ʿaniyyê*, "therefore the humble of"), while the Septuagint read them as one (*lakkənaʿanî*, "for the Canaanites"). To understand the implications of these decisions, students will need to consult biblical commentaries. Certain commentary series provide

Chart 2: Translation Variants in Zechariah 11:7a

Zechariah 11:7a NRSV	Zechariah 11:7a NAS
So, on behalf of the sheep merchants, <u>I became the shepherd</u> of the flock doomed to slaughter.	So <u>I pastured</u> the flock doomed to slaughter, *hence the afflicted of the flock.*

an author's original translations with text critical notes that can clarify such issues (for example, Word Biblical Commentary, Anchor Bible, Hermeneia, NICOT, and Augsburg Continental Commentary series). While many of these discussions require knowledge of Hebrew to adjudicate competently, beginning students will nevertheless benefit from wading through some of these notes to understand the issues involved when they encounter different translations.

Third, English translations may provide some help in determining the literary parameters of the textual unit. Many printed English translations mark their understanding of where the units change through various visual techniques. Some translations use thematic titles to mark major transition points in the text. Some use blank lines, or extra spacing between lines at the end of one unit and the beginning of another. Some begin new units with new paragraphs, but this technique is harder in prophetic texts, since most of the prophetic units are composed in poetic lines. Some translations mark new units with bold numbers. Some make no indication. Electronic texts are less consistent, since many (especially those on the Internet) make no distinction between verses beginning new units and those which do not. It therefore becomes crucial for students to understand whether and how your printed Bibles mark transitions from one unit to another. As one sees the differences in translations, one will soon need to face the question of how and why one seeks to understand prophetic texts.

The Purpose and Process of Interpretation

The primary tasks of interpretation with respect to prophetic literature are more literary in nature than they are historical, sociological, or hermeneutical. Nevertheless, because prophetic texts reached their final forms more than 2000 years ago, and because the compilation of prophetic books presumes awareness of certain events, some historical awareness has to be developed. Further, different societal structures than those of the twenty-first-century American context must be taken into account. Theological concepts and presuppositions that predate Christianity need to be understood on their own terms (to the degree that is possible) before rushing too quickly to ask the question, how is this text relevant for modern Christians? In some pedagogical contexts (e.g., many Religious Studies programs), students will explore prophetic texts merely to understand them in their ancient contexts.

Chapters 2–6 will focus upon the questions necessary for accomplishing this goal. Chapters 2–6 will focus upon the literary procedure (chap. 2), investigating pertinent historical and sociological elements (chap. 3), exploring the way in which traditional prophetic forms shed light upon the rhetoric of prophetic texts (chap. 4), analyzing a text's relationship to the larger context of the book (chap. 5), and common themes (chap. 6). These foci constitute foundational paths that will lead students to a deeper understanding of prophetic texts, within prophetic books, in their developing contexts.

It should be reiterated, and born in mind constantly, that these foci are not mechanical steps to be performed upon the text. The data and the questions that arise from these foci inform and influence one another. They offer correctives designed to help us understand prophetic texts in *their* contexts rather than forcing our assumptions onto texts written in a distant time and place. These foci also provide data that can change our perception of what a text is saying. For this reason, interpreters should reconsider how the results of the various foci enhance, challenge, and reconfigure our growing understanding of prophetic texts. These chapters, then, offer heuristic opportunities to focus on particular literary, historical, sociological, and conceptual questions, but they do not represent a linear path to a single correct interpretation.

In other contexts (e.g., most seminaries and divinity schools), students are asked to reflect upon how prophetic texts speak to communities of faith today. Chapter 6 will offer a few brief suggestions for how to begin this process responsibly, taking seriously the claims of prophetic texts and the needs of people of faith today. Communities of faith then and now are not the same, and some means of bridging the gap are necessary if one wishes to interpret prophetic texts as Scripture in modern, Christian contexts. This process involves understanding the nature and function of prophetic literature itself.

Beginning students are often surprised to learn that prophetic literature is not primarily predictive in nature. Rather, prophetic literature functions primarily as interpretive theological literature. Prophetic texts interpret personal, communal, religious, and political behavior in light of prophetic understandings of the expectations of God for God's people. In so doing, these texts also interpret history itself in light of these expectations.

Prophets, as presented in these prophetic writings, address people in crisis, whether those people know it or not. Prophetic speeches and personas confront ancient communities and powers with God's message. These confrontations use rhetoric that explicitly or implicitly challenges the hearers and readers of these texts to change their behavior. Yet most of the prophetic scrolls reached their final form at a time when the tradents were convinced that the people to whom these messages were originally addressed did not take them to heart.

Nevertheless, all four prophetic scrolls contain passages that also proclaim powerful messages of hope as well. Offering hope for something beyond the current crisis, at least for a faithful remnant, thus constitutes an important motivation for the collection and transmission of these prophetic scrolls,

even though a far larger percentage of the speeches contain words of judgment than words of hope. For this reason, one must learn to read prophetic
texts on multiple levels. One must learn to hear the individual speeches and
to separate the speeches from one another. One must, however, also learn
to hear these speeches within their current literary contexts and to recognize how they may have been adapted when they were incorporated into the
context. Finally, though, if one wishes to interpret prophetic literature as
Scripture, one must also learn to hear these texts as theological witnesses by
ancient communities of faith that deserve responsible theological reflection
for today's world.

2

Analyzing Literary Parameters and Rhetorical Flow

The need to limit the passage represents an important part of the interpretive process. Some units are independent oracles, while others function as commentary on neighboring units or help to structure portions of the book. Some units comprise lengthy passages, while others may involve only one or two lines. In each case, it helps to know where a speech or rhetorical unit begins and ends. Determining the beginning and end of significant units in prophetic texts and analyzing those units represent an important part of the interpretive process. This task typically involves multiple readings of a text for a threefold purpose: the notation of formulaic markers, delineating and classifying any change of speaker or addressee, and evaluating poetic lines and stanzas.

FORMULAIC MARKERS

Formulaic markers at the beginnings and ends of units can frequently (but not always) be detected in the presence of introductory or concluding formulas. These elements should be noted early in the process, but their presence does not guarantee a new unit has begun or ended. These elements may mark the beginning or the end of the unit, but they may also mark a transition point in a larger unit. Care must be taken to analyze how a text marker *functions* within any given context.

At least six different formulaic elements appear regularly in prophetic texts. These formulaic elements may not always be present, but if they are, they serve as strong indicators that a new speech is beginning. These formulas include (1) messenger formulas, (2) word events, (3) vision-report formulas,

(4) eschatological-day phrases, (5) "behold" + participle, and (6) "(for) YHWH has spoken."

Messenger Formulas

The messenger formula gets its name from the presumed setting that produced the formula. When a messenger read a pronouncement for a king, the messenger would begin the pronouncement by stating the authority by whom he spoke: "Thus, says the king." In prophetic literature, the authority is not a human king, but YHWH. Messenger formulas appear in each of the prophetic books, though in only half of the writings of the Book of the Twelve (the formula does not appear in Hosea, Joel, Jonah, Habakkuk, Zephaniah, or Malachi). These formulas can play different roles in prophetic texts, as introductions or transitions.

Each of the eight oracles against the nations in Amos 1–2 begins with a messenger formula (1:3, 6, 9, 11, 13; 2:1, 4, 6). In these oracles the messenger formula functions as both an introduction and a unifying element by introducing the refrain ("for three transgressions of X and for four, I will not revoke the punishment").

In other instances, the messenger formula frequently introduces the verdict in a judgment oracle (Jer. 7:20 in 7:16–20, shown in chart 3). A typical judgment oracle includes a statement of the situation, the adverb "therefore," and the messenger formula as the prophet announces YHWH's verdict.

Chart 3: Jeremiah 7:16–20

Commission to the Prophet:

[16]As for you, do not pray for this people, do not raise a cry or prayer on their behalf, and do not intercede with me, for I will not hear you.

Indication of the Situation:

[17]Do you not see what they are doing in the towns of Judah and in the streets of Jerusalem? [18]The children gather wood, the fathers kindle fire, and the women knead dough, to make cakes for the queen of heaven; and they pour out drink offerings to other gods, to provoke me to anger. [19]Is it I whom they provoke? says the LORD. Is it not themselves, to their own hurt?

Verdict (beginning "therefore" with the messenger formula):

[20]Therefore thus says the Lord GOD: My anger and my wrath shall be poured out on this place, on human beings and animals, on the trees of the field and the fruit of the ground; it will burn and not be quenched.

Chart 4: Jeremiah 6:16–19

Accusation against the People (beginning with the messenger formula):

[16]Thus says the LORD: Stand at the crossroads, and look, and ask for the ancient paths, where the good way lies; and walk in it, and find rest for your souls.

But they said, "We will not walk in it." [17]Also I raised up sentinels for you: "Give heed to the sound of the trumpet!"

But they said, "We will not give heed."

Verdict:

[18]Therefore hear, O nations, and know, O congregation, what will happen to them. [19]Hear, O earth; I am going to bring disaster on this people, the fruit of their schemes, because they have not given heed to my words; and as for my teaching, they have rejected it.

The messenger formula can also introduce the beginning of a judgment oracle, not just the verdict section, as illustrated in chart 4.

The messenger formula can also appear as a transitional element marking major thematic shifts or new sayings in collections. For example, the messenger formula appears ten times in Zechariah 8, marking the beginning of new sayings and thematic shifts (8:2, 3, 4, 6, 7, 9, 14, 19, 20, 23). As a result, every messenger formula must be evaluated to determine how it functions rhetorically in its context.

Word-Event Formulas

The second type of prophetic formula is called the word-event formula. Its name derives from its primary characteristic as an introductory pronouncement that "The word of YHWH (came) to X." The word-event formula plays two primary roles: to introduce prophetic writings (functioning as titles) and to introduce new speeches within prophetic books.

As superscriptions, word-event formulas appear at the top of scrolls and speeches, essentially functioning as titles for the text following. Sometimes these superscriptions introduce entire books, at other times only sections of books (no word-event formula appears in Isaiah until 2:1). The superscriptions at the beginning of books often provide chronological, biographical, and/or thematic data necessary for the reader to place the subsequent material into a setting. These formulas represent the work of editors who recorded traditions about the prophetic figure associated with the material.

These traditions may include chronological data, biographical information, and the subject matter to be addressed. Several word-event formulas provide chronological data in the form of the king(s) who reigned during the prophet's lifetime (see Hos. 1:1; Mic. 1:1; Zeph. 1:1) or by dating speeches to specific years in the reign of one or more kings (e.g., see Jer. 1:1–3; 25:1; Ezek. 24:1; Hag. 1:1; 2:1; Zech. 1:1,7; 7:1). Biographical information usually appears in the form of the prophet's father (Hos. 1:1; Joel 1:1; Jonah 1:1; Zeph. 1:1; Jer. 1:1–2) or the prophet's home town (Amos 1:1; Mic. 1:1; Jer. 1:1–2). Word-event formulas also occasionally mention the topic of the material following (Mic. 1:1; see Zech. 12:1).

Word-event formulas that function as speech introductions are usually shorter because they introduce individual speeches or blocks of material rather than entire books, but they can provide chronological data or separate one speech from another. In Ezekiel, Haggai, and Zechariah, the chronological data of multiple word-event formulas play a role in the shaping of the book, since the majority of the dates in these books appear in chronological order. Jeremiah, by contrast, does not display this interest in developing a consistent chronological arrangement. Chronological data in the narrative portions of Jeremiah is often provided in conjunction with various forms of word-event formulas as shown in chart 5.

Chart 5: Jeremiah Chronology

26:1	starts with the beginning of the reign of Jehoiakim (609).
27:1	tells of the beginning of the reign of Zedekiah (597).
32:1	dates the material to the tenth year of Zedekiah (597), when Jeremiah was confined.
33:1	brings a "second" word to Jeremiah during this period when Jeremiah was confined.
34:1	dates the chapter to the time when Nebuchadnezzar laid siege to Jerusalem in the reign of Zedekiah (post-598).
35:1	dates the message to the reign of Jehoiakim (609–598).
36:1	dates the confrontation between Jeremiah and Jehoiakim to the fourth year of Jehoiakim's reign (605), the year of the battle of Carchemish.
44:1	is YHWH's word to Jeremiah for those living in Egypt (which implies after the destruction of Jerusalem in 587).
45:1	dates to the fourth year of Jehoiakim when Jeremiah dictated to Baruch.
46:1	does not provide chronological data, but it begins the oracles against the nations (chaps. 46–51) with a word-event formula.

Consider Jeremiah 7:1–2a (MT), noted in the previous chapter. This short text is not present in the LXX version of Jeremiah. It is no coincidence that the insertion begins with the word-event formula ("the word that came to Jeremiah from YHWH"), because the word-event formula separates speeches from one another. The word-event formula in the MT is not present in the LXX *Vorlage*, i.e., the Hebrew source used by the translator. Its addition recognizes that Jeremiah 7:4 sets the speaker in the temple, while chapter 6 commanded the prophet to stand in the crossroads (6:16). This change helps to illustrate the function of the word-event formula to mark significant changes for the reader.

Vision-Report Formulas

A third introductory formula introduces vision reports with a variety of formulations. The narrative form of this formula implies that the prophet is recounting a visionary experience. Three examples may illustrate the use of the formula. The first two usually appear in or near the beginning of a vision report.

The first type reports YHWH as the source of a vision: "And YHWH showed me" or "he showed me" (Amos 7:1, 3, 7; 8:1; Zech. 3:1). This formula not only introduces a vision report; it also suggests an active role on the part of someone other than the prophet. In Amos, the other one involved in the vision is YHWH. Zechariah 3:1, by contrast, presumes that the messenger of YHWH accompanying the prophet on his visionary journey is the one who shows the prophet the visions.

The second variation puts more emphasis upon the visionary than upon God. "I saw" or "I looked and I saw" (Ezek. 2:9; 8:2; Amos 9:1; Zech. 1:8, 18 (MT 2:1); 2:1 (MT 2:5); 5:1, 9; 6:1). This formula, like the others, introduces a new vision report that allows the reader to see a new topic. It differs from the first formula in that it does not necessarily convey an active role on the part of someone other than the prophet who is relaying the message. Consider Amos 9:1, for example. The first four vision reports in Amos 7–8 involve YHWH showing something to the prophet. These vision reports also involve extensive conversation between the prophet and YHWH. By contrast, Amos 9:1 merely presents the prophet in the role of spectator as YHWH destroys the sanctuary. There is no dialogue, only a soliloquy in which YHWH commands the destruction to take place.

The third form introduces a conversation within a vision report: He asked me, "What do you see?" (Amos 8:2; Zech. 4:2). As a result, the conversational introduction often appears as a transitional element to move the report along when used with another formula (see Amos 8:1, 2). When this shift happens, the question often introduces a conversation about the vision itself.

Eschatological-Day Phrases

The fourth formulaic element also appears in several variations: "on that day," "in those days," and "behold, the days are coming." These formulas typically introduce an eschatological shift or a new unit by referring to some day or days in the future.

"On that day" (Heb. *bayyôm hahû*). Two characteristics are notable with units beginning with "on that day." First, the phrase *bayyôm hahû* in the prophetic corpus refers almost exclusively to things in the future. This future orientation is contrasted with the use of the phrase "on that day" in narrative texts, where it generally refers to things in the past (e.g., Josh. 4:14; Judg. 6:32), unless it involves some kind of prophetic pronouncement (e.g., Deut. 31:17–18). Second, the contexts of these introductions in the prophetic corpus are overwhelmingly promissory in nature. For example, Amos 9:11 marks a shift for the last five verses of Amos, where, for the first time, promises appear. These promises often begin a new section of promises (e.g., Amos 9:11–12, 13–15), or the formula appears in groups (e.g., Zech. 14:4, 6, 8, 9, 13, 20, 21), where it introduces new sayings on a similar topic—the day of YHWH.

"In those days" (Heb. *bayyāmîm hāhēm*) functions similarly to *bayyôm hahû*, with the exception that the plural form seems to suggest a more protracted period. This phrase is less common than "on that day," but it does appear more frequently in Jeremiah than in the other writings (Jer. 3:16, 18; 5:18; 31:29; 33:15–16; 50:4, 20; Joel 2:29 [=MT 3:1]; 3:1 [=MT 4:1]; Zech. 8:6, 23).

"Behold the days are coming" (Heb. *hinnēh yāmîm bāʾîm*) represents a third way in which these eschatological formulas appear at the beginning of new sections. It appears mostly in Jeremiah and Amos. Unlike the first two examples, this formula is not limited to introducing future promises. For example, two of the three occurrences in Amos (4:2; 8:11; cf. 9:13) provide pronouncements of judgment rather than hope.

The function of these eschatological formulas remains the most important point. They introduce chronological shifts in the context where they appear, and these shifts orient the reader toward the future. The majority of these formulas signal a time of future promise.

However, one syntactical item is often overlooked in these two eschatological formulas. Specifically, the relative pronoun ("that," "those") assumes an antecedent, and this assumption requires that the formulas relate to their literary context. For example, Amos 9:11 offers a promise that begins with "on *that* day." In its context, this promise can refer only to the deliverance of the remnant in 9:7–10. Thus it assumes the deliverance of a remnant but extends that promise well beyond the idea of mere survival, when 9:11–12 announces restoration of the Davidic kingdom. Determining the nature of the antecedent becomes important in contexts where this phrase appears.

These eschatological formulas appear more frequently in some writings than others. For example, "on that day" appears more than forty times in both the Book of the Twelve and in Isaiah, but the formula is not evenly distributed across the entire corpus. In the Book of the Twelve, the phrase "on that day" appears forty-one times in nine of the twelve writings, but twenty-two of those forty-one appear in Zechariah (though only three in Zech. 1–8). The phrase appears in Isaiah forty-five times (all except one appear in chapters 2–31). By contrast, the phrase appears only ten times in Jeremiah and thirteen times in Ezekiel. What this distribution says about the process of transmission is not entirely clear, but it does suggest that some texts focus more extensively on the future than others.

"Behold" + Participle

Another formula involved in marking new prophetic units consists of the particle "behold" (*hinnēh*) followed by a participle. The particle can appear as "behold" (*hinnēh*) or "behold, I . . ." (*hinnî*). Unlike the eschatological formulas, this formula does not indicate some idyllic point in the distant future but a divine action that will take place in the imminent future. Further, these formulas do not usually introduce independent units, but they appear near the beginning of subunits that begin a new section of a larger unit.

For example, Habakkuk begins with a prophetic complaint about the lack of justice in the land (1:2–4). A divine speech follows in 1:5–11. Following a command to look among the nations in 1:5, "for a work is being done in your days," Habakkuk 1:6 provides a more specific declaration of that work and emphasizes the nearness of that work with "Behold, I am about to raise the Chaldeans" (NRSV "For I am rousing the Chaldeans"). The remainder of the unit describes in great detail the terrifying nature of this enemy. Here, while "behold" (*hinnēh*) followed by a participle does not formally begin the divine speech, it marks the specific pronouncement of punishment and emphasizes the imminence of the attack, while the remainder of the unit contains merely descriptive statements concerning the Babylonians. Unfortunately, this formula is not always readily apparent in recent English translations, since they may use another word for "behold" (*hinnēh*), such as "look" (NET) or even omit "behold" for stylistic reasons (NRSV, NIV). Nevertheless, commentaries should refer to the phrase, because it serves the purpose of accentuating the nearness of the action.

"(For) YHWH Has Spoken"

Less common, but still significant, is the phrase "YHWH has spoken." This phrase can mark the end of a saying or larger unit. For example, the phrase marks the end of a unit in Isaiah 1:20, since 1:21 begins with a new addressee. By contrast, the same phrase marks the end of a call to attention and the beginning of a divine quote in Isaiah 1:2 but not the end of the larger unit. Careful attention must therefore be paid to the rhetorical context when this formula appears. It does, however, more frequently conclude units and sub-units than it serves as an introduction.

Significance of Formulaic Markers

The importance of these six formulaic markers comes in their potential to mark significant shifts in the text and to signal to the reader certain expectations regarding time and perspective. Several of these markers indicate that the following text involves the future. Eschatological-day phrases tend to relate to the more distant future, while "behold + participle" formulations suggest imminent action. Other formulas suggest a change in perspective or emphasize a role in the material to follow and can signal a new speech. The word-event formula generally appears at the beginning of a new speech. The messenger formula underscores the prophetic role of the speaker and affirms the speaker's authority as a representative of YHWH. It can appear at the beginning of a new speech or an important turning point in the unit, such as when it marks the verdict in a judgment oracle. Vision-report formulas signal that what follows involves elements of a vision, which will likely require interpretation. Paying attention to these formulas helps one begin to hear the units on their own terms.

CHANGE OF SPEAKERS AND ADDRESSEES

In addition to noting formulaic markers, the careful evaluation of the change of speaker or addressee provides important information for assessing the literary parameters and the function of literary units.

"Who Speaks What to Whom?"

This question is the guiding literary question for interpreting prophetic literature. The first task of the interpreter has often been described as analogous to a film director explaining a scene to the actors. Where do a given character's lines stop and start (*who speaks*)? Does one character address another directly, or does the character speak about another character (*to whom*)? *What* does the character talk about (words of judgment or deliverance; words of confrontation, admonition, or hope)?

In prophetic literature, the three characters appearing most frequently are YHWH, the prophet, and the people. Each character may function in a given text as either speaker or addressee, but other characters also play these roles in significant ways. As important as it is to recognize a change in speaker or addressee, the nature of prophetic literature requires that one must use this information to assess the significance of the change for the literary and rhetorical form of the text.

A speaker can change for several reasons. The change can indicate a new unit is beginning, but a change in speaker can also indicate the presence of dialogue, meaning that the change of speaker is still part of the same unit. Further, a formal change in speaker can occur when one speaker quotes the presumed response of another character—especially when that speaker is disputing the actions of another. For example, in Micah 7:8–10 the speaker challenges an unnamed entity who rejoices at the speaker's misfortune. This confrontation culminates in 7:10, where the speaker quotes the enemy and then refutes the enemy's quote: "Then my enemy will see, and shame will cover her who said to me, 'Where is YHWH your God?' My eyes will see her downfall; now she will we be trodden down like the mire of the streets."

Formally, the question "Where is your God?" marks an important shift in the speaker, but it does not indicate a new unit. In this instance, the text signals the change explicitly at the beginning of the question, but it is left to the reader to determine where the quote of the enemy ceases and the speech of the original speaker continues. Often prophetic texts do not provide an explicit notation indicating the change of speaker. They must be deduced.

The same can be said for addressees. The change of addressee (i.e., the identity of the person or persons being addressed) can signal that one has begun a new unit. On the other hand, this change may signal something important about the character of a unit. For example, after addressing a group using second masculine plural pronouns and verbs, a prophetic text may suddenly shift to a second masculine singular pronoun. However, if that singular pronoun refers to YHWH, then it is possible that the prophetic speech conveys an intercessory prayer on behalf of the group who had just been addressed. In this case, this change of addressee infers a continuation of a single rhetorical event rather than two separate, independent units. For example, Joel 3:9–11 (MT 4:9–11) consists largely of plural commands to convey words of judgment to the nations, but the final line of 3:11 changes to a petition to YHWH, using a singular verb, a vocative that addresses YHWH by name, and a singular pronoun. In this instance, the final phrase of 3:11 ("Bring down your warriors, YHWH") does not begin a new unit but must be interpreted as a prayer from the prophet to YHWH.

For these reasons, the careful interpreter of prophetic texts must work through each line of the passage with the goal of explaining the constellation of characters involved in a given text, as well as the relationship of those characters to the form of that same text. In other words, with each line of a given passage, the interpreter must be able to answer the question, who speaks what to whom?

God as Speaker

Many prophetic texts will state explicitly that YHWH is the speaker. Two of the more common formulas that introduce prophetic units (the messenger formula and the word-event formula) generally signal YHWH as the speaker for what follows. In most instances, YHWH's speech will be related in some way to oracular forms. In other cases, one must deduce YHWH as the speaker from the nature of the speech.

Once one identifies YHWH as the speaker, it is important to recognize and to articulate how God is speaking or being addressed. This task overlaps to a certain extent with the task of recognizing different genres (see chap. 4), but determining the explicit and implicit modes of speech represents an analytical step that actually precedes the consideration of genre. Here observations will be limited to modes of divine speech in five different arenas: oracles, visions, symbolic acts, disputations, and soliloquies.

Prophetic oracles follow two basic forms (the judgment oracle and the salvation oracle), but these are determined by their content and a variation in their literary form more than the mode of divine speech. Both types of oracles convey YHWH's speech. Nevertheless, it must be remembered that all divine speech in prophetic texts is reported speech. This reported speech can be seen most readily by the presence of those formulaic elements that introduce the oracles (e.g., the messenger formula and the word-event formula). Direct speech from YHWH, in its literary form, typically involves an explicit statement from a narrator introducing YHWH as the speaker or the use of first-person verbs and pronouns that assume YHWH as the speaker. In oracles, these speeches typically address the prophet or the people directly, though sometimes the two are blended.

Indirect speech represents instances wherein YHWH should be assumed as the speaker, or the source of the speech, even though the speech lacks formal indicators to this effect. It can be difficult to distinguish the prophet from YHWH in these instances.

Jeremiah 2:5–9 offers a good case in point, especially in relation to its context. This oracle, like many judgment oracles, begins with a messenger formula ("Thus says YHWH"). The speaker subsequently uses first-person-singular pronouns and verbs in 2:5, 7–9, as well as a citation marker in 2:9 (*nəʾum-yhwh*) emphasizing YHWH as the speaker. These verses thus consistently report the words as YHWH speech. Nevertheless, twice within this unit YHWH quotes the speech of someone else. YHWH quotes the speech of the ancestors in 2:6 and the priests at the beginning of 2:8. These quotes represent an example of indirect speech, since their words are recounted but YHWH speaks them. This oracle culminates in 2:9 with YHWH's pronouncement of judgment (introduced by "therefore," as in most judgment oracles).

By contrast, Jeremiah 2:14–19 uses a series of rhetorical questions to accuse the people of wickedness, but these questions refer to YHWH and God in the third person (2:17–19). On the surface, then, one would assume the speaker is the prophet formally. However, the very end of 2:19 switches to first-person divine speech ("The fear of *me* is not in you, says the Lord GOD of hosts"). The fact that this quote is marked by the same citation marker indicating YHWH as the speaker that appeared in 2:9 highlights the stylistic change of the first-person speech. Yet the question remains as to how to interpret this fluctuation of formal style. Evaluating such changes is never easy or without debate, but it seems plausible here to suggest that this oracle wants the reader to equate the words of the prophet with the words of YHWH. In other words, many oracular forms assume that a genuine prophet's words are indeed delivered at the behest of YHWH. In these instances, the oracles become a kind of indirect speech of YHWH, even though formally the prophet must be conceptualized as the speaker.

Visions, or more accurately vision reports (see chap. 4), generally require a different set of assumptions from the reader when one encounters first-person divine speech. Often these vision reports involve reported conversation, so that "I" speeches may alternate between YHWH and the prophet. In this case, one should not equate the speech of the prophet with that of YHWH. To illustrate, consider Amos 7:7–9 in chart 6 on page 28. One must pay careful attention to the changing speakers, because both YHWH and the prophet speak in the first person. Here the new speaker is introduced, but this explicit note is not always present.

Symbolic acts convey a command directly from YHWH to the prophet, with the expectation that the command will be executed in order to make a point to the people. For example, Ezekiel 21:18–24 begins with a word-event formula followed by a command from YHWH to the prophet to draw a sign depicting a road forking in two different directions (21:19–20). This command gives way to an explanation of the sign (21:21–23) that begins with "for"

Chart 6: Amos 7:7–9

This is what he showed me [*the prophet*]: the Lord was standing beside a wall built with a plumb line, with a plumb line in his hand. [8]And the LORD said to me [*the prophet*], "Amos, what do you see?"

And I [*the prophet*] said, "A plumb line."

Then the Lord said,

> "See, I [*YHWH*] am setting a plumb line in the midst of my [*YHWH*] people
> Israel; I [*YHWH*] will never again pass them by; [9]the high places of Isaac
> shall be made desolate, and the sanctuaries of Israel shall be laid waste, and I
> [*YHWH*] will rise against the house of Jeroboam with the sword."

---

or "because" (Heb. *kî*) before concluding with a pronouncement of judgment (21:24), which itself begins with the messenger formula. In this instance, the symbolic act recounts YHWH speech directly to the prophet without ever using a first-person verb or pronoun that refers to YHWH. Rather, the narrator specifies YHWH as the speaker (21:18, 24). These two formulas provide the symbolic act with divine authority, while the reported discourse allows the reader to overhear an intimate conversation between YHWH and the prophet, which simultaneously conveys an important message to the reader: namely, YHWH, not the Babylonian king, chose to destroy Jerusalem.

Disputations frequently use direct indirect speech from YHWH, blended with speech from the prophet and indirect speech from the people. Consider Malachi 1:2–5 in chart 7, where YHWH speaks but quotes both the people and Edom, in order to get the people to change their perspective from questioning YHWH to affirming YHWH's magnificence.

The goal of changing the attitude of the people involves the framework of a formal speech by YHWH, who quotes what the people have said at the beginning (1:2) and what YHWH hopes that people will say at the end of the disputation. In between, YHWH puts forward a programmatic statement ("I have loved Jacob") and its converse ("I have hated Esau"), followed by a more specific illustration of what that means for the Edomites (considered the descendants of Esau). In this example, one must deduce the addressee primarily from the frame addressing the people, not the quotes.

Divine soliloquies, though less common than oracles and vision reports, represent yet another mode of speech, wherein YHWH speaks to YHWH, but the text presumes that the reader/hearer will "listen in" on the conversation in order to learn something about YHWH. Hosea 11 offers a classic example of this speech form. YHWH consistently speaks in the first person about Ephraim (the name for the northern kingdom used in Hosea), addressing Ephraim directly only in 11:8–9. Despite the direct address to Ephraim using second-masculine-singular pronouns, most scholars would treat these

Chart 7: Malachi 1:2–5

> [2]I have loved you, <u>says the LORD</u>. But you say, "How have you loved us?"
>
> Is not Esau Jacob's brother? <u>says the LORD</u>.
>
> Yet I have loved Jacob [3]but I have hated Esau;
>
> I have made his hill country a desolation and his heritage a desert for jackals. [4]If *Edom* says, "We are shattered but we will rebuild the ruins,"
>
> <u>the LORD of hosts says</u>: They may build, but I will tear down, until they are called the wicked country, the people with whom the LORD is angry forever.
>
> [5]Your own eyes shall see this, and *you shall say*, "Great is the LORD beyond the borders of Israel!"

references as examples of indirect address. These second-person references should be interpreted as the musings of YHWH more than evidence of a conversation. They function within a larger unit where YHWH speaks to YHWH.

God as Addressee

In addition to God speaking in various prophetic forms, one must also pay attention to the ways God is addressed. As noted above, God may appear as a conversation partner in vision reports and symbolic acts, but the role of God as addressee may also involve liturgical forms and constructed dialogue.

Liturgical Forms

Three examples of liturgical forms that may address YHWH directly in the context of prophetic collections can be given here, though these examples are by no means exhaustive. These forms include prayer, psalms of various types, and prophetic liturgies.

Prayer can be addressed to YHWH by either the prophet or the people. The prophetic speaker most commonly prays in the form of petition. For example, in the first two visions of Amos (7:1–3, 4–6), immediately after seeing a vision of horrendous devastation, the prophet intercedes on Israel's behalf: "O Lord GOD, forgive, I beg you! How can Jacob stand? He is so small!" (7:2, 5). In both instances, the petition leads to a change of heart on YHWH's part. By contrast, the third vision (7:7–9) leads to a portrayal of imminent destruction, but the prophet does not intercede. Rather, one finds a narrated confrontation between Amos and Amaziah, the chief priest at Bethel (7:10–17). Ironically, this narrative conveys the priest's decision to expel Amos from the land, the same prophet who had just interceded twice with YHWH on Israel's behalf. In this case, both the language of prayer and its absence add to the interpretation of the vision reports.

God may be addressed in psalms of various types, and these psalms can be placed in a prophetic context, even though these psalms were not originally composed for this purpose. The psalms may be slightly revised to integrate them to some degree into their new setting, but it is not always clear that this has occurred. Examples of the use of psalmic material include the thanksgiving hymns in Isaiah 12 and Jonah 2 and the theophany hymns in Nahum 1 (which was also originally a semiacrostic poem) and Habakkuk 3. Each of these hymns addresses YHWH directly, at least in reported speech, but the forms of address reflect the hymn genre more than a prophetic genre (see chap. 4).

The psalmic material usually plays a thematic function within the prophetic book, and the address of YHWH directly does not usually convey a dialogue. Nevertheless, the thematic function of the psalm may be quite important for the structure of the book, since these psalms often occur at key junctures. For example, the psalms in Nahum and Habakkuk begin and end their respective writings, while Isaiah 12 appears at the end of a major block in Isaiah, just before the beginning of the oracles against the nations in Isaiah 13. In these instances, the interpreter should work to understand the psalm as an independent piece before attempting to describe its secondary function in its prophetic context. Both contexts are important when one is trying to understand the final form of the text.

A prophetic liturgy may also include sections that address YHWH directly. A prophetic liturgy consists of a series of sayings from different speakers that usually coalesce around a common theme. These sayings convey some degree of logical progression or linguistic interplay between the units. This connective element is what characterizes the series as a liturgy rather than a simple collection of sayings grouped together because of their common theme. For example, Micah 7:8–20, shown in chart 8, contains five subunits dealing with salvific promises, but these subunits may contain more than one speaker (see 7:8–10 and 7:14–15).

Of course, one will find that commentators debate the extent of the inherent unity of the sayings that comprise the liturgy and even question whether

Chart 8: Micah 7:8–20

Micah 7:8–10	Lady Zion speaks to Lady Nineveh (whose response is both reported and refuted).
Micah 7:11–13	responds to Lady Zion.
Micah 7:14–15	contains a prophetic prayer of intercession (7:14–15a) and YHWH's brief response (7:15b).
Micah 7:16–17	presents a prophetic address to the people.
Micah 7:18–20	conveys the people's response in the form of a hymnic prayer.

the term represents an anachronism. Nevertheless, even if one decides that this "liturgy" represents a composite piece, the interpreter's job does not stop until one has reflected upon why someone has combined these pieces in this location in the book.

Constructed Dialogue

Closely related to the use of liturgical elements, constructed dialogue can be a formal presentation of two or more independent units that are placed alongside one another for a rhetorical purpose, to give the impression that one unit responds to the other. Certain passages involve units whose placement suggests an editorial concern to present a response from YHWH, even if that response does not reflect the inherent compositional style of the material to which it responds.

Here an illustration will suffice. Habakkuk 1:2–4 begins the book with an individual complaint. A prophetic figure speaks in the first person directly to YHWH, expressing agitation at the state of the prophet's society, where violence and injustice have become the norm. The oracular material that follows (1:5–11) begins immediately thereafter with a speech from YHWH, also using a first-person style (see 1:6). This divine speech contains no messenger formula or other formulaic introduction to indicate a change in speaker. Rather, whereas the individual in 1:2–4 addressed YHWH directly, and the prophet used an autobiographic style to refer to himself ("I, me"), the "I" in 1:6 cannot be the prophet, because the activity described (rousing a nation) is not a task performed by humans. Further, this oracular unit begins with a command in 1:5, which distinguishes itself from the interrogatives in 1:2–4; but this command is addressed to a group, not to an individual. This change is unmistakable in Hebrew, though hardly evident in English, where the imperative form is identical for commands given to individuals and to groups.

One can also debate whether or not Habakkuk 1:5–11 represents the original response to the questions posed by the prophet in 1:2–4, but the answer to this question is not the end of the interpretive process. Whether 1:5–11 represents an originally independent oracle or a communal response to an individual, most interpreters recognize that its position following the complaint language in 1:2–4 almost certainly represents an editor's desire to interpret 1:5–11 as YHWH's response to the prophet's complaint. On the editorial level, then, the prophet complains that the land has become rife with wickedness and injustice (1:2–4), while YHWH announces his intention to bring the Babylonians to destroy the land (1:5–11). The complaint functions as the accusation, while the oracle pronounces judgment. Unfortunately, not every example of changing style between units can be explained as clearly. Caution must be exercised against overinterpreting the meaning of one unit next to another.

The Prophet as Speaker and Recipient

Despite the prominence of oracles and other forms that draw upon divine first-person speech, YHWH is not the only speaker in prophetic texts. In the ongoing task of determining who speaks what to whom, one must carefully evaluate the role of the prophet as speaker in order to describe the attributes of a given passage. The prophet can speak to and with YHWH, on the one hand, or the people, on the other. The characters engaged in the text, and the role they play in that engagement, go a long way toward understanding the dynamics of the passage.

Prophet as Speaker

The figure of prophet in the Old Testament texts functions primarily as the mouthpiece for God. Whether explicitly or implicitly, most texts presume that the prophetic speaker carries the imprimatur of YHWH's messenger. One sees this role as intermediary quite clearly in those oracles introduced by the messenger formulas. When the text explicitly says, "Thus says the LORD," a divine speech usually follows. In formal terms, however, one must conceptualize the prophet as the speaker of the messenger formula.

Recognizing this role as intermediary helps to account in some texts for the frequent vacillation between YHWH speaking in the first person and the prophet speaking about YHWH in the third person. The role of intermediary was such an integral part of the prophetic persona that sometimes the two roles fuse with one another. For example, consider Amos 5:4–7. These verses containing two short sayings (5:4–5, 6–7) that parallel one another in terms of content. The only real distinguishing characteristic separating the first part from the second part is that YHWH speaks in 5:4–5 ("Seek me and live"), while the prophet speaks about YHWH in 5:6–7 ("Seek the LORD and live"). As intermediary, the prophet conveys YHWH's message to the people.

Prophet as Recipient

In addition to the prophet speaking, the prophetic unit may also report discourse in which the prophet functions as the recipient of a message from YHWH. Often, of course, the prophet recounts these events in order to convey a particular message to those reading the text. This style of address plays a particularly prominent role in Ezekiel and Jeremiah, where it often serves as a vehicle for communication in vision reports (e.g., Jer. 24:1–10), when introducing symbolic acts (e.g., Ezek. 12:1–6), or when reporting internal discourse from YHWH (e.g., Ezek. 3:1–11 and the confessions of Jeremiah). In these instances, direct address to the prophet comes from YHWH, underscoring the authority of the prophet and the intimate relationship between

Chart 9: Jeremiah 11:18–20

> [18]It was the L̲O̲R̲D̲ who made it known to me, and I knew; then you showed me their evil deeds. [19]But I was like a gentle lamb led to the slaughter. And I did not know it was against me that they devised schemes, saying, "Let us destroy the tree with its fruit, let us cut him off from the land of the living, so that his name will no longer be remembered!" [20]But you, O L̲O̲R̲D̲ of hosts, who judge righteously, who try the heart and the mind, let me see your retribution upon them, for to you I have committed my cause.

the prophet and God. Moreover, these passages generally refer to the people in the third person, which creates a certain distance between YHWH and the people. They may be mentioned in indirect discourse or presumed as onlookers when recounting internal dialogue. For example, consider the opening verses of the so-called confessions of Jeremiah (11:18–20), shown in chart 9.[1]

These verses recount YHWH's revelation of betrayal to the prophet (11:18–19) followed by the prophet's prayer to YHWH for retribution against those who plotted against him (11:20). The reader is not told the identity of this group, but in its current location this encounter introduces the judgment oracle against the men of Anathoth that follows (11:21–23). Thus the internal dialogue explains the situation that evoked the pronouncement of judgment against Anathoth.

An important task, therefore, when interpreting prophetic units is to attempt, insofar as possible, to determine the extent to which any given unit assumes the prophet as a character in his own right. Is the message of the text conveyed in a form whereby the prophet serves primarily as YHWH's mouthpiece, or does the text report a vision or dialogue wherein the prophet must be clearly distinguished from YHWH because the prophet interacts with YHWH?

The People as Addressees and Speakers

The third primary character in prophetic units is the people, who usually appear collectively as the addressee of a divine or prophetic speech. Not infrequently, however, the people also speak to the prophet or to YHWH. Sometimes a text will delineate explicitly the people's role as speaker and addressee, making it easy to see these changing roles, as in Jeremiah 18:7–11 in chart 10 on page 34.

In 18:11, YHWH commands the prophet to relay a message to the people. YHWH's speech addresses the prophet with a singular command ("say"), then states the content of the message addressing the people using second-masculine-plural pronouns. Even if one does not know Hebrew to see the changing pronouns, the explicit introductions of the speeches allows one to detect the change of speaker.

Chart 10: Jeremiah 18:7–11

---

[11]Now, therefore, say [singular] *to the people* of Judah and the inhabitants of Jerusalem:

> Thus says the LORD: Look, I am a potter shaping evil against you [plural] and devising a plan against you. Turn now, all of you from your evil way, and amend your ways and your doings.

[12]But *they* say,

> It is no use! We will follow our own plans, and each of us will act according to the stubbornness of our evil will.

[13]Therefore thus says the LORD:

> Ask [plural] among the nations: Who has heard the like of this? The virgin Israel has done a most horrible thing. [14]Does the snow of Lebanon leave the crags of Sirion? Do the mountain waters run dry, the cold flowing streams? [15]But my people have forgotten me, they burn offerings to a delusion; they have stumbled in their ways, in the ancient roads, and have gone into bypaths, not the highway, [16]making their land a horror, a thing to be hissed at forever. All who pass by it are horrified and shake their heads. [17]Like the wind from the east, I will scatter them before the enemy. I will show them my back, not my face, in the day of their calamity.

Further, in 18:12, YHWH recounts to the prophet what the people will say when they reject YHWH's admonition to cease their wicked behavior. Formally, the speaker changes, but this is reported speech that serves to document their rejection of YHWH. This rejection of YHWH by the people then leads to another speech by YHWH (18:13–17). The speech is first addressed to the people (note the plural command "ask") using a series of rhetorical questions (18:13–14). However, as YHWH turns to accusation (18:15) and pronounces judgment (18:16–17), YHWH speaks *about* the people in the third person, a style more typical of the judge pronouncing a verdict.

In Jeremiah 18:11–17, the citation formulas at the beginning of the first three verses aid the reader as the speaker changes. However, even here readers of the text must analyze the flow of the passage to determine the addressee in 18:14–17 (especially in English, which does not distinguish the singular "you" from the plural "you"). To accomplish this analysis with confidence, students who do not know Hebrew will need to rely upon critical commentaries, biblical software, or reliable Web sites containing interlinear analyses of the Hebrew and English text.[2] Such analysis should be a foundational task for the interpreter of prophetic texts. Much confusion can result when one does not pay careful attention to the changing speakers and addressees in each line of a prophetic text. The subject of every verb and every pronoun should be clear to the interpreter before he or she attempts an explanation of a given text.

Unfortunately, not every prophetic text provides the reader with citation formulas like those in Jeremiah 18:11–13. Frequently, speakers and/or addressees change with no warning, leaving the reader with the task of deducing these changes from the variation of subjects, pronouns, and the action described. The absence of such formulas complicates the task, but identifying the speakers and addressees remains a necessary component of interpreting prophetic texts.

Other Characters

In addition to YHWH, the prophet, and the people, prophetic texts frequently introduce or presuppose other characters in speeches, confrontations, promises, or narratives. These characters must be analyzed contextually for the way they function in the text, based upon typical assumptions, explicit statements, and external data. Such characters include various royal and religious functionaries, Lady Zion, and other aids and foils.

Royal and Priestly Functionaries

Cultic and royal functionaries can play distinctive but wide-ranging roles in prophetic texts. Priests, kings, princes, governors, and other officials can be cited or presumed in prophetic units. These functionaries may be cited as a group or named as individuals. Consider the interplay of the three characters Amaziah, Jeroboam, and Amos in the prophetic narrative found in Amos 7:10–17. These three characters represent a priest, a king, and a prophet, but these personages are not value-neutral in this context. Amaziah is called "the priest from Bethel," which implies he should be understood as the chief priest. In Amos, however, Bethel consistently comes under fire as a place of cultic malpractice, so that the reader associates the chief priest with these poignant accusations (3:14; 4:4; 5:5–6). In fact, the narrative quickly confirms that Amaziah functions as an antagonist to Amos, since Amaziah represents Amos as a brigand who is out to destroy Israel and its king (7:10–11). When Amaziah describes the temple at Bethel as "the king's sanctuary" and the "temple of the kingdom," one can hardly understand these epithets as anything other than sarcasm, since the temple should belong to YHWH. Further, the king, Jeroboam II, appears only offstage as the recipient of Amaziah's letter and the object of the prophet's condemnation (see 7:9). As a result, the narrative subtly portrays the king as weak and overtly presents the chief priest as hostile to YHWH's spokesperson. These assumptions add considerable texture to the brief literary portrayal of this confrontation, the more so since it is the prophet, and not the priest, who has twice interceded to YHWH on behalf of Israel in the first two vision reports of this chapter (7:2, 5).

Lady Zion

Lady Zion represents a significant character in each of the four prophetic books (Isaiah, Jeremiah, Ezekiel, and the Twelve). In West Semitic cultures of the ancient world it was not unusual to find cities personified as women, often as female deities married to the primary male god of the region. The prophetic adaptation of this tradition lies behind the appearance of Lady Zion in prophetic texts.[3] Lady Zion's appearance is easily recognized in Hebrew because the feminine pronouns and verbal forms used to speak to or about her are distinct from the masculine pronouns typically used when referring to the country or the people. The significance of this extended metaphor is twofold.

First, in Old Testament texts, this idea is adopted to convey an intimate relationship between YHWH and Lady Zion, though she is never portrayed as a goddess. The relationship between YHWH and Lady Zion is presupposed metaphorically to be that of husband and wife, not unlike the metaphor in Hosea 2, where the land is personified as the wife of YHWH. Lady Zion is not only wife but also mother. Her children in these extended metaphors represent the people of Jerusalem.

Second, and relatedly, Lady Zion is not some amorphous character but connotes the city of Jerusalem and its environs. Frequently prophetic texts where Lady Zion appears allow topoi to be discussed wherein YHWH's role in the fate of the city can be separated from the question of the fate of the people. In this constellation, Lady Zion is often portrayed as having children, and these children represent the inhabitants of the city. Her care for these children often provides the implicit motivation for her actions or speeches. At other times, descriptions of Lady Zion's appearance in prophetic texts allow authors to depict Jerusalem's past glory by describing the way that Lady Zion used to look.

Consider a passage from Isaiah that draws upon these two assumptions of the extended metaphor. Isaiah 49:14–23 offers an excellent example of how this constellation of metaphors may function, wherein Lady Zion is presumed to be wife and mother, on the one hand, and the city of Jerusalem, on the other. Following a call to rejoice addressed to both the people and the land (49:13), YHWH recognizes the suffering of Lady Zion, who has not yet been restored (i.e., rebuilt and resettled). YHWH quotes her accusation, in which she essentially accuses YHWH of being a deadbeat dad, abandoning her and her children: [14]"But Zion said [fs], 'The Lord has forsaken me, my Lord has forgotten me.'"

In response, YHWH draws an analogy between his own love for Lady Zion and the love that a mother feels for her nursing child: [15]"Can a woman forget her nursing child, or show no compassion for the child of her womb?

Even these may forget, yet I will not forget you [fs]." YHWH then speaks directly to Lady Zion, offering her a promise to rebuild her and to return her children that she thought were orphaned:

> [16]See, I have inscribed you [fs] on the palms of my hands; your [fs] walls are continually before me. [17]Your [fs] builders outdo your [fs] destroyers, and those who laid you [fs] waste go away from you [fs]. [18]Lift up your [fs] eyes all around and see; they all gather, they come to you [fs]. As I live, says the LORD, you [fs] shall put all of them on like an ornament, and like a bride you [fs] shall bind them on.
>
> [19]Surely your [fs] waste and your [fs] desolate places and your [fs] devastated land—surely now you [fs] will be too crowded for your [fs] inhabitants, and those who swallowed you [fs] up will be far away.
>
> [20]The children born in the time of your [fs] bereavement will yet say in your [fs] hearing: "The place is too crowded for me; make room for me to settle."
>
> [21]Then you [fs] will say in your [fs] heart, "Who has borne me these? I was bereaved and barren, exiled and put away—so who has reared these? I was left all alone—where then have these come from?"
>
> [22]Thus says the Lord GOD: I will soon lift up my hand to the nations, and raise my signal to the peoples; and they shall bring your [fs] sons in their bosom, and your [fs] daughters shall be carried on their shoulders. [23]Kings shall be your [fs] foster fathers, and their queens your [fs] nursing mothers. With their faces to the ground they shall bow down to you [fs], and lick the dust of your [fs] feet. Then you [fs] will know that I am the LORD; those who wait for me shall not be put to shame.

This passage simply cannot be understood if one does not recognize that Lady Zion functions as an integral part of the conversation. The prophetic rhetoric using this metaphor often assumes or makes explicit that Lady Zion has been sent away, or exiled, because she was unfaithful to YHWH. This rhetoric can appear quite harsh, as the prophets often portray her as a prostitute or an adulteress when accusing her of breaking the marital covenant. Two things should be noted in this respect. First, setting aside the role of gender in the metaphor, these accusations against Lady Zion are no more violent than many of those directed against the people when masculine metaphors are used. Many prophetic texts portray YHWH's judgment in personal terms directed against the people or Lady Zion. This very graphic and violent imagery certainly repulses many today when they read the Old Testament (but such violent images of God are also not lacking in the New Testament).

Second, especially given the patriarchal nature of ancient culture, one should not miss the fact that Lady Zion appears in prophetic texts just as frequently as the subject of promises as the subject of judgment. This is not accidental. The prophetic writings are frequently concerned with documenting the reasons for judgment as well as proclaiming that the relationship between YHWH and YHWH's people continues. In prophetic texts, especially those at the end of the writings, YHWH frequently takes the initiative to restore the people, the land, the cities, and YHWH's relationship with Lady Zion.

Other Aids and Foils

In various prophetic texts, one will encounter additional characters whose relationship to the context, the prophet, and God requires careful analysis. The appearance of these additional characters happens more frequently in prophetic narrative literature than in its poetic texts. However, additional characters may appear in poetic texts as well. One particular class of poetic texts, for example, requires the presence of an additional character within the constellation of speakers, addressees, and objects. Oracles against foreign nations appear in all four prophetic scrolls, usually in poetic texts (Isa. 13–23; Jer. 46–51 [=25–31 in LXX]; Ezek. 25–32). These nations may be addressed directly; they may speak for themselves (albeit usually in rather politically charged quotes); or they may be the object of a given oracle and thus appear only in the third person. Often the oracles against foreign nations in a prophetic scroll or writing are compiled together so that one might find several originally independent sayings about a single country adjacent to one another.

While the role of the nations in oracles against foreign nations is almost always hostile, additional characters in narrative texts need to be evaluated on a case-by-case basis. These additional characters may serve as protagonists or antagonists in a given context, meaning that their speech and their actions need to be assessed accordingly. For example, Baruch, Jeremiah's amanuensis, plays a prominent role in chapters 32–45. He is clearly a trusted ally of the prophet who faces considerable danger because of his relationship to Jeremiah. By contrast, Amaziah, the chief priest of Bethel, challenges the prophet with harsh words in Amos 7:10–17 (as noted above).

Interestingly, and extremely significantly for understanding the purpose of the narrative, the foreigners in Jonah run counter to type. Whereas in the prophetic oracles against foreign nations, the nations were always hostile, that is not the case in Jonah. The readers of Jonah 1 would assume the sailors were foreigners because they are worshiping different deities (1:6), but these foreign characters end up worshiping YHWH (1:16). Further, the dreaded Assyrians, once Jonah finally arrives in Nineveh, respond dramatically to Jonah's petulant five-word sermon (3:4). They repent, proclaim a fast, and put on sackcloth (3:5). In fact, their conversion is so complete that, by the time word of it reaches the king, all that is left for him to do is to include the animals in his official proclamation (3:7–8).

These additional characters can be human or nonhuman. In addition to the role of cattle in Jonah 3, one may encounter entities from the heavenly host as the warriors of YHWH (Joel 3:11) or as an interpreting angel (Zech. 1:9). Prophets can refer to beings in a vision, such as the two women with wings like a stork who carry away a third woman, representing evil, to a foreign land (Zech. 5:5–11).

The wide variety and function of these ancillary characters is far too extensive to cover adequately in this context. What is important for the interpretive process when one encounters these additional characters is the assessment of how the character functions within the context. Are they hostile or friendly? Are they other human beings or symbolic entities? Do they convey the message from YHWH, or do they oppose it? Such questions will help the interpreter to understand the role played by these characters.

READING LINE BY LINE

So far, contemplation of the literary tasks has involved the analysis of two relatively formal criteria: formulas that frame the units and identifying the speakers and addressees. The third task of the literary process is to read the unit line by line. Often, this task is itself integrally involved with the first two tasks of determining the literary parameters in the speakers/addressees of a given unit. Thus, while reading each line of the prophetic unit constitutes a third task, these three tasks should be conceptualized as overlapping procedures, not sequential acts. The important task of reading line by line focuses heavily upon three key goals: identifying signs of parallelism, explaining the identity of every pronoun and verbal subject, and analyzing the syntactical connectors between the lines.

Identifying Signs of Parallelism

Various types of parallel expressions are a key characteristic of Hebrew poetry used with most prophetic oracles. Since the work of Bishop Lowth in the eighteenth century, scholars have sought to classify various types of parallelism. The following selections are intended to be illustrative, not comprehensive.[4] Three types of parallelism can usually be detected in English translations (synonymous, antithetical, and stair-step). A fourth type (chiastic) is harder to detect, because it depends upon word order as well as parallel elements, and the word order in English may be different than in Hebrew. Nevertheless, it will be briefly mentioned here.

Synonymous Parallelism

Synonymous parallelism occurs when syntactical formulations repeat, using synonyms or similar imagery to extend the idea being expressed. These syntactical formulations may include entire sentences, two or more poetic lines, or individual parts of speech repeated to achieve this effect. Chart 11 below, which shows Isaiah 30:8–14, will help illustrate several types of parallelism.

One can readily see synonymous parallelism in the first two lines of Isaiah 30:8. Three syntactical elements parallel one another in these two lines: the

Chart 11: Isaiah 30:8–14

[8]Go now, write   it before them on a tablet,
        and   inscribe it   in a book,
           so that it may be   for the time to come
                                                as a witness forever.

[9]For they are
        a rebellious people,
           faithless   children,
                        children who will not   hear the instruction of the LORD;

[10]   who say   to the seers,   "Do not see";
                             and   to the prophets, "Do not prophesy to us what is right;
                             speak to us   smooth things,
                             prophesy   illusions,

[11]   leave   the way,
                             turn aside from   the path,
                        let us   hear no more about the Holy One of
                                                Israel."

[12]Therefore thus says the Holy One of Israel:
        Because you reject   this word,
            and   put your trust in oppression and deceit,
            and   rely   on them;

[13]therefore this iniquity shall become for you
        like a break in a high wall,
                bulging out,
                and about to collapse,
                whose crash comes   suddenly,
                                       in an instant;

[14]   its   breaking is like that of a potter's vessel
        that is smashed so ruthlessly
        that among its   fragments
                 not a   sherd is found   for taking fire from the hearth,
                                           or dipping water out of the cistern.

verbal command (write/inscribe); the direct object ("it" repeated twice); and a prepositional phrase (on a tablet/book). The compounding of these statements should not be understood as two separate commands resulting in two different written documents but as one command expressed artistically and poetically.

Similarly, images related to a single syntactical element appear explicitly four times in five lines in 30:9–10 ("people"/"children"/"children"/"who"). The first two of these lines contain parallel adjectives ("rebellious"/"faithless") that modify the subject nouns, thus describing the people/children. The next three lines use parallel images to describe what this group does (they refuse instruction and tell YHWH's visionaries to stop prophesying).

Antithetical Parallelism

Antithetical parallelism uses antonyms and contrasting images across multiple lines or syntactical elements in order to extend the idea being expressed. One can readily see this mode of expression in lines two and three of Isaiah 30:12. There the verbs ("reject"/"trust") and the objects ("this word"/"oppression and deceit") use contrasting terms to broaden the accusation against YHWH's people. In so doing, they portray the people not merely falling short of YHWH's expectations but actively opposing those expectations.

Stair-Step Parallelism

Stair-step parallelism uses synonymous or antithetical parallels across multiple lines while simultaneously showing some type of progression in the thoughts being discussed. For example, in Isaiah 30:12 we already noted the antithetical parallelism in lines two and three, but lines three and four are linked by synonymous parallelism between the two verbs ("trust"/"rely") and the objects ("oppression and deceit"/"them"). Thus lines two through four in 30:12 are connected to one another with two different kinds of parallelism, but these links also convey a progression of activity. The people reject YHWH's word, but not apathetically. Rather, they act in opposition to YHWH's word by actively trusting in oppression and deceit. Line four takes this behavior a step further. By speaking about relying upon oppression and deceit, this line implies a level of continuity of action, thus connoting a pattern of behavior rather than a single act of rebellion.

Similarly, consider the repeated and progressive elements in the imagery of the wall in Isaiah 30:13–14. The NRSV's rendering of the MT refers to the break in a high wall and then recognizes the interplay of participles in 30:13, which refer to that breach as bulging, collapsing, and crashing. The visual image of destruction is compounded by the speed with which this crash occurs ("suddenly," "in an instant"). These two images give way to a new metaphor in 30:14, to describe the destruction in terms of pottery. It assumes that the reader/hearer knows that a piece of pottery, when dropped normally, will break; but the larger pieces were kept for very utilitarian functions (carrying hot coals and scooping water from the cistern into a larger container). However, the description of the crash is compared to a potter's jar that is shattered so violently that no big pieces are left that could even perform this function

Chiastic Parallelism

Chiastic parallelism represents another stylistic variation on the use of parallelism. Chiastic parallelism involves the use of parallel elements where the parallel elements appear in reverse order than the order in which those elements first appeared. If, for example, three elements are repeated in chiastic style, these elements would be labeled A-B-C/C-B-A. As with the other types of parallelism, the parallel elements may appear as synonyms or antonyms; the parallel elements may include a mixture of nouns and verbs. Chiasm says much about the artistry with which prophetic poetry was composed, but since it is based upon Hebrew word order, it is often difficult to recognize in English translation. Frequently the word order in Hebrew must be changed when translated into English, because English syntactical constructions require a different order. To illustrate, consider Isaiah 30:8a. The NRSV puts the relevant portion into smooth English: "Write it before them on a tablet, and inscribe it in the book." As already noted, this line uses synonymous parallelism in terms of the words themselves. However, the English translation cannot convey the Hebrew word order, which actually unfolds in a chiastic pattern that includes five elements whose order would be A-B-C-B-A, as shown in chart 12.

One can see this chiastic pattern in a literal translation, but this artistic word order in Hebrew often becomes stilted or cumbersome in English. Translations will typically give preference to English style rather than to Hebrew word order.

The parallel elements need not be limited to repetitions of specific words. Sometimes one even finds syntactical alternations, meaning that the parts of speech in the sentence may form the parallels. In these instances one may

Chart 12: Isaiah 30:8a

A			Write it	kotbāh
	B		upon a tablet	ʿal-lûaḥ
		C	for them	ʾittām
	B		and upon a book	wə ʿal-sēper
A			inscribe it	ḥuqqāh

find, rather than synonyms or antonyms, chiastic parallels in the structure of two sentences containing the syntactical pattern (e.g., verb-subject-object/ object-subject-verb). These are much more difficult to illustrate, since none of the English translations can consistently render these elements in English.

Explaining the Identity of Pronouns and Verbal Subjects

It is not normally difficult to identify the subjects and pronouns, but it is a crucial step in the interpretive process for answering the question, who speaks what to whom? In quite a number of prophetic texts, however, identifying the subjects and pronouns can be a matter of debate or interpretation. The reasons for the uncertainty can be linguistic or conceptual.

Linguistically, interpretive decisions often have to be made, because Hebrew has no neuter pronoun. Every noun must be either masculine or feminine. English pronouns function quite differently, since English pronouns referring to things require "it" rather than "he" or "she." Further, the gender of Hebrew nouns is not always logical. For example, in Hebrew the word "rock" (ṣûr) is masculine but the word "stone" ('eben) is feminine. English translations will use "it" to refer to both, because the neuter pronoun is required in English.

However, in some instances, translators must interpret for the reader which Hebrew pronouns refer to which nouns, and these decisions can cause debate. Even more commonly, English pronouns create confusion or mask problems in the Hebrew text. The most common example of this confusion comes with the second-person pronouns. Hebrew has four different pronouns for "you" (2ms, 2mp, 2fs, 2fp). The single choice of "you" for English pronouns, then, cannot convey the complexity of speakers and addressees in passages conveying conversations. For example, in Habakkuk 1:2, the prophetic voice utters a complaint to YHWH directly: "YHWH, how long shall I cry for help and *you* [2ms] not listen?" This direct address continues until 1:5, when YHWH "responds": "Look among the nations and see! Be astonished! Be astounded! For a work is being done in *your* days that *you* would not believe if *you* were told." This response appears seamless in English but less so in Hebrew, because the verbs and pronouns are all plural, while one would presume YHWH would answer the prophet using singular pronouns. This unexpected change to plural raises questions: Who else should the reader assume is present? Does this "response" represent an independent source (1:5–11) placed here for rhetorical reasons? Or does 1:2–11 represent an original composition in which the prophet speaks to the LORD but the LORD responds to the people as a group?

Such questions arise naturally from the Hebrew text, but the answers to these questions are debated. Interpreters will need to evaluate such problems

Chart 13: Nahum 1:12–14

¹²Thus says the LORD,

"Though they [3mp] are at full strength and many, they will be cut off and pass away.

Though I have afflicted you [2fs], I will afflict you [2fs] no more.

¹³And now I will break off his [3ms] yoke from you [2fs] and snap the bonds that bind you [2fs]."

¹⁴The LORD has commanded concerning you [2ms]:

"Your [2ms] name shall be perpetuated no longer;

from the house of your [2ms] gods I will cut off the carved image and the cast image.

I will make your [2ms] grave, for you [2ms] are worthless.'"

with the help of good scholarly commentaries. To illustrate further, consider the changing pronouns in Nahum 1:12–14 in chart 13.

If the reader does not analyze these lines carefully, they are a confusing jumble of contradictory statements in English. However, by carefully noting the changing gender and number of the addressee, the reader sees that two different entities are being addressed in these verses. On the one hand, the "you" (2fs) receives a promise that judgment is ending ("Though I have afflicted you [2fs], I will afflict you [2fs] no more"). The punishment has come from a masculine singular entity ("his yoke"), which, given the context, refers to the king of Assyria. By contrast, it makes good sense if one thinks of the "you" whose punishment will be ended—given the possible constellations of addressees—as Lady Zion (Jerusalem personified). On the other hand, the "you" (2ms) in Nahum 1:14, who is now the subject and addressee of a judgment speech, is the king of Assyria, who had been the instrument of oppression ("his yoke," "bonds"). Thus, the central message becomes consistent. YHWH will remove Zion's punishment and the king of Assyria will not survive. In the case of Nahum 1:12–14, knowing the conceptual realia available to prophetic poets makes sense of the changing pronouns, which in turn makes sense of an otherwise nonsensical series of statements.

Analyzing the Syntactical Connectors between Lines

Evaluating the syntactical connectors represents a third key task for interpreting prophetic lines. Sometimes these connectors may serve as a crucial marker for the rhetorical flow in particular genres (see the discussion of "therefore" in judgment speeches in chap. 4). At other times, this task is less dramatic, but equally important. These connectors relay to the reader such syntactical functions as causality ("for," "because"), chronology ("then," "at that time,"

Chart 14: Past or Future Act in Joel 2:18

Joel 2:18 (NRSV)	Joel 2:18 (NIV)
Then the LORD *became* jealous for his land, and *had* pity on his people.	*Then* the LORD *will be* jealous for his land and *take* pity on his people.

"on that day"), and concessive statements ("if," "though"). These functions must be analyzed on a case-by-case basis, and multiple English translations should be consulted to determine at least four different possibilities: (1) the nature of the syntactical connector (e.g., simple conjunction, *vav* consecutive, or concessive); (2) the extent of its connective function (e.g., dependent clause or connecting two paragraphs); (3) whether more than one option is plausible; (4) what difference the variation makes for understanding the text.

To illustrate, consider Joel 2:18 in its context, as shown in chart 14.

These two translations represent two possible understandings of a syntactical connector. The chief difference between the two understandings concerns when to place the action of the verb. The NRSV places it in the past (as do the Tanak and the NET). The NIV places the action in the future (so also KJV, NKJV, and NASB). The nature of the syntactical connector is a conjunction. The word "then" translates the Hebrew conjunction *vav*, having a common, but particular, form. This particular form of the conjunction (called a *vav* consecutive) has two primary functions, to show sequence ("and then") or consequence ("and as a result" or "so that"). The extent of the connective function is pivotal for understanding the entire second chapter of Joel. The preceding verses, Joel 2:12–17, have implored the people of Judah and Jerusalem to repent in the hopes that YHWH will change YHWH's mind about sending the attacking army described in 2:1–11. Those translating 2:18 as past emphasize the conjunction's sequential nature, and they interpret 2:18 as a report of YHWH's beneficent action *on the presumption* that the people have done exactly as they had been commanded in 2:12–17. Those translating 2:18 as future accentuate the conjunction's consequential function, and they interpret 2:18 as the anticipated promise of what YHWH will do *on the presumption* the text has not specifically stated that the people actually did as implored in 2:12–17.

In this instance, both options carry some degree of plausibility, because in actuality there is a gap in the text that requires the interpreter to supply information: namely, how do the people react, or do they react, in response to the call to repentance? Those who think the reader is supposed to *assume* the people responded positively become more likely to see 2:18 as YHWH's response to the people's response. For them, the remainder of the chapter then becomes a report of a series of blessings that YHWH provides to these people who have responded to the call to repent. On the other hand, those translating 2:18 as future tend to *assume* that the author would have provided the people's response, if they had indeed made one. Consequently, they consider 2:18 and the remainder of the chapter as future blessings that YHWH is prepared to provide if and when the people do repent. Thus, these four elements can be answered in more than one way, and these answers result in very different interpretations of Joel 2:19–27. For one set of interpreters, the remainder of the chapter functions as promise fulfilled or at least in process; while for the other set of interpreters, 2:19–27 represents potential promise, one contingent upon a response not yet in evidence.

3

Selecting Key Words

The references to people, places, and things are not value-neutral in prophetic and poetic texts. They often convey attitudes, presume knowledge, and impart values that are not necessarily stated explicitly. This chapter will illustrate some of the ways in which places, people, and theological terms add depth and texture to prophetic texts, once interpreters learn to recognize their value and begin to explore the many tools available for building a knowledge base to aid in the interpretive process.

PLACES: GEOGRAPHY, TOPOLOGY, LOCATION

The importance of understanding a prophetic text can often be enhanced by the simple discipline of locating countries, towns, or other places on a map. For example, the comedic qualities of Jonah become recognizable very quickly when, in the first three verses, YHWH commands Jonah to go Nineveh (several hundred miles to the east) and Jonah responds by hiring a boat taking him toward Tarshish (several hundred miles across the Mediterranean Sea in the opposite direction). Amos opens with a motto that summarizes the theme of the writing: "The LORD roars from Zion, and utters his voice from Jerusalem; the pastures of the shepherds wither, and the top of Carmel dries up" (1:2). One can hardly understand the significance of this statement if one does not realize that Carmel represents the highest peak of Israel, the northern kingdom. Amos 1:2 juxtaposes Carmel over against Jerusalem, and the metaphors of the verse imply God's judgment upon Israel while emphasizing the priority of Jerusalem's temple mount in comparison to the high point of Israel. These images effectively summarize the message of the book, since Amos stems from Tekoa (a small village just outside Jerusalem), and the vast majority of the speech material in this book pronounces judgment against the northern kingdom. Perhaps, for those who know the story, the fact that 1 Kings 18 narrates Elijah's confrontation of Ahab and defeat of Baal as having taken place on the mountain at Carmel adds a polemical nuance that colors this one little hymnic verse with a poignancy that fits quite well with much of the stinging tone of the speeches in Amos.

PLACES: ASSOCIATIVE MEANINGS

The mention of cities and towns should be evaluated for their prominence, their political associations, and the historical situation in which the text is set. Capital cities often connote a sense of power, real or potential, in prophetic texts, but these are not the only ways that places function within poetic texts. Ancient authors and readers often attribute certain characteristics or attitudes to particular towns or villages, but modern readers may or may not be immediately aware of those connotations. For example, most modern readers instinctively treat a reference to Washington, DC, differently than they would the mention of Hodgenville, Kentucky. Nevertheless, a careful reader would understand the potential symbolic value of the latter, much smaller village if they knew that this little town was the birthplace of Abraham Lincoln. Thus size alone is not the only reason that cities and villages may appear in prophetic texts.

The relative prominence of villages, towns, and especially capital cities should be incorporated into the interpretive process of poetic texts in particular. Cities may be symbols of political power, of past glory, or of attitudes held by the author of a given text. For example, Jerusalem and Samaria may symbolize Judah and Israel respectively, because these were the sites where the king's palace existed. However, Jerusalem in particular often conveys more emotive power than most modern readers would associate with a capital city. The composition of no small number of prophetic texts shows that they are imbued with an awareness of the Zion tradition.

The Zion tradition represents a kind of worldview through which writers experience their surroundings and articulate their concerns. In practical terms, texts related to the Zion tradition typically deal with some combination of three themes: YHWH's choice of Jerusalem as the place of worship, Jerusalem as the center of the ongoing Davidic monarchy, and YHWH's protection of Jerusalem from the nations. The way in which these three motifs work their way into individual texts varies widely. For example, Isaiah 11:10–16 represents a fairly typical text in this respect, since it involves all three elements of the Zion tradition. Its reference to the "root of Jesse" alludes to the restored prominence of the Davidic king whom foreign nations will consult (11:10) and portrays YHWH's restoration of the country by YHWH's menacing actions toward a number of specific foreign nations (11:12–16). In so doing, the text *presumes* the reader knows that YHWH starts from Jerusalem.

In Joel 3:18 [MT 4:18], one finds Judah and Jerusalem combined with "Wadi Shittim" in a symbolic statement. This text makes a promise that "all the streambeds of Judah shall flow with water" and "a fountain shall come forth from the house of YHWH and water the Wadi Shittim." The symbolic power of Shittim becomes clear when one learns that according to Joshua 2:1 and 3:1, Shittim is the place where the Israelites camped before crossing the Jordan after forty years of wandering in the wilderness. Thus the poetic image conveys a sense of promise for abundant water for the entire land, from Shittim on the far side of the Jordan to the Temple Mount in Jerusalem.

Political associations may also be important as background information about places. Nineveh was the capital city of Assyria at the time that Samaria was destroyed (722 BCE) and Sennacherib, king of Assyria, laid siege to Jerusalem (701 BCE). Assyria became the regional superpower that dominated the region, including Judah and Israel, until Babylon destroyed Nineveh in 612 BCE. This background information is essential knowledge if one is to understand the vehemence with which the book of Nahum condemns Nineveh. Assyria dominated Judah as a foreign power for so long and destroyed the capital city of Israel, meaning that it came to symbolize foreign occupation and oppression.

On the other hand, knowledge of this symbolic function of Nineveh—especially when combined with chronological and archaeological data about this city—serves to highlight the hyperbole embedded in the story of Jonah in order to emphasize YHWH's compassion. Nineveh serves as a symbolic representation of evil because of the long-standing hatred of its occupation of Judah. Nevertheless, the size of Nineveh described in the book of Jonah presumes a much larger city (a three day's journey according to Jonah 3:3) than its archaeological remains would suggest, since the entire circumference of the city was only about seven miles (a distance that could be readily walked in three to four hours). Of course, such hyperbole is typical of the author's comedic style, given that the author portrays sailors as a righteous, pious lot (Jonah 1) and the king of Assyria as one who shows his concern for the repentance of Nineveh's cattle as well as its people (3:8). The point of this hyperbole in Jonah, however, has a serious theological purpose. The book aims its pointed barbs at people like Jonah, who think that God's compassion should be limited to God's people, while foreigners should be treated with hostility (4:2–3, 9–11).

Chronology may even play a role in understanding the symbolic function of a town. Staying with the example of Nineveh, one can understand the long-standing power such symbols can accrue when one incorporates the results of critical scholarship with the history of Nineveh. The prophet Jonah is mentioned in 2 Kings 14:25 as a court prophet who prophesied during the reign of Jeroboam II (786–746 BCE). For many reasons, however, scholars tend to date the book of Jonah to the late Persian or even the early Hellenistic period. This date occurs roughly four or five centuries after the prophet for whom the book is named. Moreover, in the time of Jeroboam II, Nineveh was not yet the capital of Assyria. Yet this late compositional date for Jonah also means that Nineveh still functioned as a powerful symbol of foreign oppression more than two centuries after the city was destroyed in 612 BCE. Clearly the political legacy of Assyrian hegemony survived long after its actual political power.

PEOPLE

Good Bible dictionaries provide an excellent source of information for quickly determining where else in the Hebrew Bible a person mentioned in a prophetic text may appear. For example, the book of Hosea opens by telling the story of the prophet having three children by the prostitute Gomer. Each child is named so as to serve as a message for Israel. The first child is named Jezreel, "for in a little while I will punish the house of Jehu for the blood of Jezreel" (Hos. 1:4). One will have a hard time understanding the meaning of this name if one does not know that Jehu was the king of Israel who came to power through an insurrection that overthrew King Ahab. Further, and quite importantly, Jehu's insurrection, according to the story, involved the betrayal of killing seventy male descendants of Ahab in the city of Jezreel (1 Kgs. 10:1–11). Of course, this knowledge raises interesting interpretive questions, since the narrative in 1 Kings 10 relays this act, and Jehu's insurrection itself, quite positively, because it results in the elimination of Ahab, whom the editor of Kings views as the worst king in Israel's entire history (1 Kgs. 16:30). By contrast, the symbolic act in Hosea presupposes that the prophet and YHWH condemn the actions of Jehu, not praise them. Here one sees a distinctive tension between the presuppositions of Hosea, a northern prophet, and those presuppositions of the editors of Kings, who routinely reject anything associated with the kings of the northern kingdom. Thus the way that references to people function in prophetic texts may or may not be consistent from one book to the next.

KEY TERMS

Theological terms and concepts about God or God's character often play a pivotal role in the presuppositions and the theological claims of prophetic texts. Such terms may rely upon or modify similar ideas from the cultural context of the ancient Near East in general, or they may be peculiar to Israel or Judah.

Concepts

Significant theological concepts are frequently expressed with words that exhibit a range of meanings, often interconnected, that require translation by several different English words, depending upon the context. A good case in point is represented by the concept of justice, often used to translate the Hebrew word *mišpāṭ*. The word *mišpāṭ* has a broad array of meanings, as illustrated by the various words used to translate it and the varied contexts where *mišpāṭ* appears. These meanings include "statute," "justice," "right," and "punishment."

The word *mišpāṭ* often refers to instruction for behavior and consequently is translated "statute." These instances comprise many of the examples of the word as used in the Torah (see Deut. 6:1). These statutes also include admonitions against actions that keep people from doing what is proper, and this idea of doing the right thing is also *mišpāṭ*. Such action includes admonitions to judges against taking bribes (Deut. 16:18–20). The concept of justice was not limited to those who could afford to pay for it. Rather, judges should administer justice to all (*mišpāṭ*). Justice was also expected to be available for marginalized groups like the resident alien, the poor, the needy, widows, and orphans (see Deut. 24:14, 17). Hence, Amos 5:12–15 accuses the house of Israel of taking bribes and pushing aside the needy in the gate (5:12) on the presumption that they are breaking such statutes. Amos 5:15 challenges the people, instead, to "establish justice (*mišpāṭ*) in the gate." In so doing, the text assumes the breaking of "statutes" means the lack of "proper order," both meanings of *mišpāṭ*.

Similarly, the word *mišpāṭ* may refer to a claim or the expectation of a legal right to do something. Such is the case when a relative of Jeremiah sells a field. He approaches Jeremiah because Jeremiah has the legal "right" to purchase the field (Jer. 32:7). This "right" is also the word *mišpāṭ*.

Further, the word *mišpāṭ* can also mean "punishment" in contexts of judgment, because to impose *mišpāṭ* in a certain context requires punitive action in order to set things right (see Jer. 4:12, for example).

Finally, *mišpāṭ* can also be translated as "justice" when it is used to describe ideal behavior in human relationships—in other words, doing what is right and proper toward one another. Two very famous passages illustrate this nuance beautifully, because they reject religious practices designed to appease YHWH when these practices are not closely connected with ethical behavior. In Amos 5:21–24, YHWH rejects religious festivals, sacrifices, and songs unless and until the people "let justice (*mišpāṭ*) roll down like waters, and righteousness like an everflowing stream" (5:24). Micah 6:6–8 speaks of the absurdity of the idea that animal sacrifice, or human sacrifice, will move YHWH, when all YHWH really wants is for people "to do justice, to love kindness, and to walk humbly with your God" (Mic. 6:8).

Hence, the context—social and literary—must be investigated carefully to understand how this one word, *mišpāṭ*, can mean so many different things. Such is the nature of language in general, but one should also note that a similar phenomenon exists for the English word "justice." It can refer to restitution in a legal case, as when someone seeks justice in a civil case where one party claims to have been wronged. It can also refer to retaliation, as when someone "exacts justice" upon another. Moreover, "justice" also refers to a universal ideal of that which is right and fair, as when we speak of truth and justice as societal norms. One has to learn to detect the idioms and the contexts in which the same word can connote different ideas. Often, these ideas are more interconnected conceptually than one might realize at first glance. Such is clearly the case with the Hebrew word *mišpāṭ* and the English word "justice."

Beginning students will not always be aware of the Hebrew word used in a particular context, but they will encounter various translations of a Hebrew word that reflect different interpretations of the various nuances of that word. At this point, commentaries will be helpful in finding the Hebrew word so they can decide for themselves which nuance fits best in a given context. For example, one can come across translations that differ on the meaning behind a given word, as in Isaiah 9:6, where some versions translate *mišpāṭ* as "justice" (NRSV, NIV, NASB) and others translate it as "judgment" (KJV, NKJV).

Metaphors, Similes, and Analogies

Using human language to describe God always involves inexact and incomplete linguistic approximations. Nevertheless, the poetic mind-set utilized in prophetic literature allows the presentation of God in metaphorical imagery that can and should be explored when interpreting texts. William Brown, in *Seeing the Psalms*, helpfully describes the ways in which metaphors function by referring to the source and target domains of the words involved in a compar-

Chart 15: Target and Source Domains

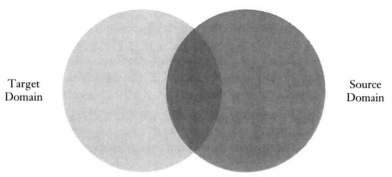

Target
Domain

Source
Domain

ison or analogy.[1] He correctly notes that metaphors do not function linearly. Rather, each word connotes a range of associations, some of which are more appropriate and meaningful than others in a given comparison. The range of meanings associated with the source domain of one word, when mapped onto the target domain (i.e., the range of meanings associated with the other word), allows the interpreter to draw actively from the interpreter's own knowledge base in order to explore how the two domains overlap with one another to create meaning, as illustrated in chart 15.

This metaphorical language can be explicitly expressed, or it can be assumed from the description of God in specific contexts. In both instances, the interpretive value has a major impact on one's understanding of the text. Consider, for example, the metaphor of God as potter in Jeremiah 18:1–11. The metaphor is created when God commands Jeremiah to watch the potter at work (18:1–4); the account of that experience is followed by an analogy linking the actions of God with the actions of the potter, who can destroy the vessel that he is making if it turns out to be deficient in the eyes of the potter. The analogy then leads to a call to repentance from YHWH, lest YHWH turn against the vessel that he has made, namely, Judah.

At first glance, this metaphor appears rather narrowly focused upon the power that the potter holds over the vessel. However, if one takes the imagery seriously, questions arise that open up other interpretive avenues. Consider three examples. First, one can legitimately ask the question of purpose. One does not normally assume that a potter sets about making something in order to destroy it. Rather, one assumes that the potter goes about this work to create something utilitarian and probably aesthetically pleasing as well. Hence, when YHWH says in 18:11, "Look, I am a potter shaping evil against you," the reader is forced to confront a piece of the analogy that does not comport well with the purpose of a potter. This confrontation likely deepens the reader's predisposition that YHWH's people have done something terribly wrong.

Second, if one has spent much time at all watching a potter, one will know that a good potter can correct a wide range of "flaws" without having to demolish the vessel entirely. Scraping, rubbing, and wetting the clay can erase blemishes so that they are no longer visible. Smashing the vessel and starting over, once it has begun taking shape, implies a serious structural flaw that will destroy the vessel when it is placed in the kiln. When a piece of pottery explodes in the kiln, the brittle, dry shards can rarely serve any utilitarian function. Nor does anyone find these remains aesthetically pleasing. Starting over, by contrast, still leaves the potter with clay that can be reshaped and remolded. Thus the image of the potter willing to start anew adds a different slant to the image of God the potter.

Third, the image of the potter and the clay in this context also creates a certain dissonance that requires exploration. To put it bluntly, the clay has precious little to say about what it becomes. If the potter decides it will be a pot, the clay cannot decide to be a vase. Why, then, does Jeremiah 18:11 use this analogy of the clay as a lead-in to a call to repent and change? Is the disjuncture here an oversight on the part of the author, who is so focused upon the image of the potter that he overlooks the image of the clay? Or could the disjuncture be intentional, in order to heighten the juxtaposition of the image? The clay, an inanimate lump of dirt, is called to make a choice that can affect one's own fate. The language of metaphors, similes, and analogies in poetic and prophetic texts, when taken seriously, often creates dynamic interpretive avenues that beg to be explored.

Metaphors for God are not always explicit in texts.[2] For example, the vision in Isaiah 6 never specifically calls YHWH king, but the scene itself demands that one make this connection. YHWH sits upon the throne (6:1) and is served by beings in his retinue (6:2). This implied metaphor colors the entire passage, as the king's holy presence fills the room (6:3) and causes the prophet to be painfully aware of his own inadequacy (6:5). After being cleansed (6:6), the prophet volunteers to go on a mission for the king, to act as the king's messenger (6:8).

A caveat should be noted here. The presumption of the same metaphors in different texts does not mean that the two texts presume the same things concerning that metaphor. Consider the metaphor of God as judge that lies behind Micah 6:1–16 and Joel 3:9–17 (MT 4:9–17). While both texts presume an image of YHWH as judge in a courtroom scene, the presumption of how the trial unfolds is quite different in the two texts, and both differ quite substantially from what contemporary American readers would conjure up in their minds about a court case. Both the reason for judgment and the conceptualization of the scene itself reflect different scenarios in these two texts, though both presume a metaphor of YHWH as judge. In Micah 6, YHWH functions as prosecutor and judge, certainly a very different constellation than most modern readers would assume when one mentions a courtroom setting or a trial speech. Micah 6:1–2 presents the opening call to attention and the pronouncement that YHWH has a lawsuit (*rîb*) against his own people (6:2b). YHWH then begins to lay out the case against Israel, carefully delineating what YHWH has done for the people (6:3–5) before accusing them of crimes against one another (6:9–12), addressing directly the city and its assembly (6:9). At this point YHWH begins to function as judge rather than prosecutor, as he pronounces the *verdict* against the defendant, a verdict that involves desolation and famine (6:13–16).

YHWH's role as judge functions quite differently in Joel 3:9–17 (MT 4:9–17). Here the object of judgment is the nations rather than YHWH's people, and their crimes must be *deduced* from the conclusion of the passage, which describes YHWH as a refuge for his own people (3:16 [MT 4:16]) who refuses to allow foreigners to possess Jerusalem (3:17 [MT 4:17]). The scene begins with the proclamation of a call to battle sent to the nations (3:9–10 [MT 4:9–10]), but this battle turns out to be nothing less than an eschatological battle against YHWH, who functions as both judge and executioner. The battle takes place in an imaginary valley (3:11–12 [MT 4:11–12]): the valley of Jehoshaphat (a name that means "YHWH will judge"). It is there that YHWH announces he will sit as judge (3:12 [MT 4:12]). YHWH's judgment is all but assured against the nations, since the end of this scene changes the name of the valley to another symbolic name, translated variously as the valley of decision (i.e., verdict) or cutting (3:14 [MT 4:14]).

A PROPHETIC COLLECTION'S
DISTINCTIVE CHARACTERISTICS

Significant terms in a book can add to one's theological perception of the book and/or the tradents of the book. When one speaks of tradents, one typically means the group responsible for transmitting the corpus. Sometimes, the tradents may have been the disciples. At other times, the groups responsible may have been temple prophets, and eventually scribes, in the employ of the temple. These terms or phrases need not be unique to be significant for understanding the emphases of one tradent compared to another. Such recurring terms can provide insight into characteristic themes of a corpus.

God as the "Holy One" or the "Holy One of Israel" appears thirty-one times in Isaiah.[3] This term never appears in the Torah and appears no more than twice in any other book in the Nebiim.[4] Interestingly, this characteristic expression for God appears in all three portions of Isaiah (chaps. 1–39; 40–55; 56–66), providing a certain sense of continuity to the corpus as a whole, even though the term is far more prevalent in the first two sections of the book than in the final section.

The book of Isaiah uses the word servant(s) forty-nine times, with more than two-thirds of the occurrences appearing in chapters 40–66, where the role of YHWH's people and their leaders as servants plays a major thematic function. By contrast, the entire Book of the Twelve uses the word only sixteen times, but ten of those appear in the last two writings (Zechariah and Malachi). Concordances and commentaries are immensely helpful in tracing the (re)appearance of words and phrases across prophetic writings, but care must be exercised in how one uses this data. For example, the Hebrew word 'ebed (servant) appears forty-nine times, but this, by itself, does not tell the whole story, since in these forty-nine instances the word sometimes means "slave," sometimes "minister," and sometimes "servant." This means that not every instance of "servant" is related to the broader theme.

4

Literary Forms and Rhetorical Aims

All cultures across time share a similar phenomenon in that recurring rituals, or repeated linguistic formulations, lead to recognizable patterns of speech and/or connote certain settings. These patterns may reflect mundane, ordinary settings that everybody recognizes, or they may reflect moments of high ritual. Consider, for example, what happens in a modern American context if a speaker stands up and begins a speech, "Dearly beloved." Nearly everyone in that room will immediately think of a wedding, even if the actual setting is different. Or consider what people think when they hear the phrase, "Hi, I'm not here right now . . ." People invariably think of voice mail messages. This recognition happens because of repetition. People become programmed to associate certain phrases with certain settings. We recognize these clues in our own culture because they are part of our own experience. However, when dealing with biblical texts, we often have to reconstruct recurring speech patterns and the settings to which they point, if possible, because we are simply too far removed in time and space from the shared cultural experience that they reflect. This chapter will seek to illustrate some common recurring forms in prophetic literature in order to show how recognition of these patterns can influence one's understanding of the texts.

POETRY AND NARRATIVE

The majority of material within the prophetic writings is typically classified as more poetic than narrative. Nevertheless, narrative passages can be found in all four prophetic books (Isaiah, Jeremiah, Ezekiel, and the Book of the

Twelve). Generally, the plotlines help students to follow the logic of narrative passages, though one must still work through the procedures described in chapters 2 and 3 when working with narrative texts.

The extent and the function of prophetic narratives vary greatly from book to book in the prophetic corpus. For example, Isaiah 36–39 represents one of the few narrative passages in the book of Isaiah, and it consists largely of material that parallels 2 Kings 18–20 (as well as 2 Chr. 30–32). By contrast, most of the material in Jeremiah 26–52 consists of narrative episodes about the prophet's life, though many of these narratives quote oracular material that is poetic in nature. Ezekiel also contains quite a bit of report-like material, while its vivid imagery and modes of expression often bring its formulations as close to poetry as to narrative.

In other words, it is not always possible, or necessary, to distinguish clearly between poetry and narrative. Students can generally determine whether scholars classify a passage as narrative or poetic by the way in which it is printed in most English Bibles. Narrative texts are written in normal prose lines that are typically justified on both the left and the right edges. Poetic texts, by contrast, are printed in poetic lines, meaning that the right side will have a jagged appearance, because each new poetic line will start back at the left margin.

Still, even prophetic narratives often contain oracular, poetic speeches from the prophet within a narrative episode. For example, Amos 7:10–17 consists of a narrative recounting the confrontation between Amos and Amaziah, the chief priest of Bethel. This confrontation, however, climaxes with the speech by Amos that follows the pattern of a typical judgment oracle (see 7:16–17). Thus the narrative itself largely functions to provide the context for delivering an oracle.

Prophetic oracular material, however, is not all cut from the same cloth. Prophets spoke different messages on different occasions, and these speeches often draw upon patterns that have a long history. An awareness of the variety of these patterns helps readers of prophetic literature to follow the logic of the text, so the following discussion will provide a very brief introduction to eight different prophetic forms. This list is not exhaustive but illustrative. While the following examples have been chosen for clarity, among other things, one must realize that the recognition of these forms should not result in a reading process that is looking for a checklist of genre components. Both the prophets themselves and the collection processes that led to the books as we have them have created variations to the traditional patterns. Nevertheless, recognition of the patterns significantly aids the process of reading and interpreting texts.

JUDGMENT ORACLES

The judgment oracle represents the most prominent form in prophetic literature. It appears frequently in prophetic narratives as well as in collections of prophetic sayings. The judgment oracle proper can generally be recognized by its structure and its characteristic markers. The structure and markers of a judgment oracle work together to create a rhetorical logic explaining the rationale and the punishment anticipated in a message of judgment. The judgment oracle can be delivered against an individual or a group, but the structural movement remains relatively consistent in either case. The four structural components that comprise a judgment oracle (introduction, indication of the situation, pronouncement of judgment, conclusion) essentially function as vehicles for a rhetorical logic. Each of these components can take more than one path when performing similar tasks.

The first part of a judgment oracle, the introduction, generally draws the reader's attention to the prophet or to the addressee. In narrative contexts, the introductory material can include a short commission address to the prophet or a longer narrative that sets the stage. When this introductory material appears within a preserved poetic oracle itself, this introductory material may include a brief call to attention, such as "Hear this . . . ," or it may begin with the messenger formula ("Thus says YHWH . . .").

In the second part of the judgment oracle, the indication of the situation often serves double duty as an accusation, thus providing the rationale for the judgment to follow. Sometimes the situation can be addressed by a rhetorical question. At other times, this element can be recognized by its characteristic phrasing, "because you have . . ."

The pronouncement of judgment of the oracle represents the third, and often the most extensive, component. In some ways, one can also think of this component as the verdict following an accusation, but judgment oracles do not always assume a juridical setting proper. This component is most easily recognized by the frequent presence of "therefore" just prior to the pronouncement of judgment. "Therefore" is not always present, but it is very common.

The fourth element of the judgment oracle, the concluding characterization, often supplies either a descriptive element involving the motive for YHWH's action, a statement indicating the result of the oracle, or some kind of concluding formula. This element is not always present, because the judgment oracle had a long history as a genre and in oral settings was frequently delivered as an ad hoc reaction to a given situation. By contrast, the written record of a judgment oracle sometimes transitions into another unit.

Consider the judgment oracle at the end of Amos 7:10–17. Rather than a concluding characterization after Amos's judgment oracle against Amaziah, the next verses convey the fourth vision report, one that proclaims that the end of Israel has arrived. In this location, the fourth vision report makes a more powerful statement than a conclusion to the judgment oracle would have done following the verdict of 7:17. Also, as with most genre categories in the Old Testament, the judgment oracle reflects a pattern of speech. One should not think of a genre as a list of speech components that a prophet must make sure to include while speaking officially.

Isaiah 28:14–18 and Jeremiah 28 offer two illustrations of texts where the component elements of a judgment oracle can be readily seen, in part because of the narrative contexts in which they are embedded. Isaiah 28:14–18 contains all four elements of the judgment oracle. The placement of the oracle comes immediately after a unit (28:9–13) that confronts a particular group with its inability to follow YHWH (note the refrain in 28:10, 13). The judgment oracle likely represents an independent saying, but one whose current location has been editorially connected to the preceding context by the addition of "therefore" (lākēn) right before the call to attention. This syntactical link likely provides insight into how an editor/compiler intended the unit to be read, as judgment upon those confronted in 28:9–13. Both the original setting of the oracle and its current placement ultimately deserve attention, but in chart 16 we are concerned only with noting the elements of the judgment oracle present in 28:14–18 as a means to following the rhetorical flow of these verses.

Following the opening word "therefore" (lākēn), the prophetic speaker in 28:14 expresses a call to attention that includes the command to "listen" and names the addressees of the oracle ("you scoffers who rule this people in Jerusalem"). This group reflects the leadership of Jerusalem, meaning that the prophet is challenging those in power. The indication of the situation begins, as do many judgment oracles, with "because" (kî), followed by a quote attributed to the scoffers mentioned in 28:14. This quote functions as the accusation. Its language has a rhetorical edge designed to portray the actions of these people as arrogant, deluded, and dangerous. They confess in a way that is both ambiguous and clear. They claim to have made a covenant, not with YHWH, but with death and with Sheol. Whatever this means, it cannot be good. They have deluded themselves into thinking that the impending judgment will spare them. They believe that this covenant will provide them refuge and shelter.

The verdict (28:16–17) announces YHWH's actions. This component begins rather typically with "therefore" (lākēn), followed by the messenger formula, though it contains a compound epithet for God ("thus says

Chart 16: Isaiah 28:14–18

1) Call to Attention:	[14]Therefore hear the word of the LORD, you scoffers who rule this people in Jerusalem.
2) Indication of the Situation (and Accusation):	[15]Because you have said, "We have made a covenant with death, and with Sheol we have an agreement; when the overwhelming scourge passes through it will not come to us; for we have made lies our refuge, and in falsehood we have taken shelter";
3) Verdict:	[16]therefore thus says the Lord GOD, See, I am laying in Zion a foundation stone, a tested stone, a precious cornerstone, a sure foundation: "One who trusts will not panic." [17]And I will make justice the line, and righteousness the plummet; hail will sweep away the refuge of lies, and waters will overwhelm the shelter.
4) Conclusion (Result):	[18]Then your covenant with death will be annulled, and your agreement with Sheol will not stand; when the overwhelming scourge passes through you will be beaten down by it.

YHWH Elohim"). Here the prophet's role of speaking for God becomes identified with the words of God as the prophet switches to first-person-singular speech, quoting YHWH directly. YHWH announces two actions. First, YHWH will lay a cornerstone that will serve as a genuine symbol of hope. Second, YHWH will rebuild the city with justice and righteousness by sweeping away the "refuge" and "shelter" in which the delusional leaders now trust. Notice how, in this case, the language of the verdict ironically takes up the language of "refuge" and "shelter" as the object of judgment when the accusation had used these terms as expressions of comfort for the deluded rulers.

Finally, the conclusion of the oracle (28:18) announces the results of YHWH's action by once again taking up language from the quote of the rulers by referring to the "covenant with death" and the "agreement with Sheol" mentioned in 28:15. However, in keeping with the rhetorical aims of the judgment oracle, while the speakers in 28:15 claim to have made this covenant, YHWH annuls it in 28:18. Thus the verdict and the concluding statement of the oracle completely reverse the deluded speech of the rulers in 28:15. The picture that develops is that of a prophet speaking truth to power, proclaiming hope that justice and righteousness will replace oppression and delusion.

Jeremiah 28 constitutes an extended narrative episode of Jeremiah's confrontation with Hananiah. The chapter tells the story of this encounter, which involves five distinct speeches (28:2–4, 5–9, 11, 13–14, 15–16), two by each prophet and one by YHWH. The first speech by Hananiah (28:2–4) offers what is essentially a salvation oracle (see below). The first speech of Jeremiah (28:5–9) presents a hopeful but somewhat skeptical response. Hananiah's second speech (28:11) reports the reason for Hananiah's symbolic act, essentially reiterating the promise of the first speech. Hananiah's attributes his speech, however, to YHWH, even though clearly Hananiah speaks the words. Following a brief narrative transition (28:12), YHWH addresses Jeremiah (28:13–14). Jeremiah's final speech (28:15–16) and the narrative elements that surround it (28:12–14, 17) exhibit all the formal characteristics of a judgment oracle, some even appearing twice, as shown in chart 17.

Interestingly, the two parts of the judgment oracle function together to condemn Hananiah, both for what he did and for what he said. In other words, this judgment oracle responds to both of Hananiah's speeches. YHWH's speech addressed to Jeremiah about Hananiah (28:13–14)

Chart 17: Jeremiah 28:12–17

Narrative Transition:	12Sometime after the prophet Hananiah had broken the yoke from the neck of the prophet Jeremiah, the word of the LORD came to Jeremiah:
Commission:	13Go, tell Hananiah,
Accusation #1:	Thus says the LORD: You have broken wooden bars only to forge iron bars in place of them!
Motivation:	14For thus says the LORD of hosts, the God of Israel:
	I have put an iron yoke on the neck of all these nations so that they may serve King Nebuchadnezzar of Babylon, and they shall indeed serve him; I have even given him the wild animals.
Narrative Transition:	15And the prophet Jeremiah said to the prophet Hananiah,
Call to Attention:	"Listen, Hananiah,
Accusation #2:	the LORD has not sent you, and you made this people trust in a lie.
Verdict:	16Therefore thus says the LORD: I am going to send you off the face of the earth. Within this year you will be dead, because you have spoken rebellion against the LORD."
Conclusion:	17In that same year, in the seventh month, the prophet Hananiah died.

effectively condemns Hananiah for the actions described in 28:10–11. The motivation of 28:14 even names Nebuchadnezzar and all the nations from Hananiah's speech in 28:11. By contrast, the judgment oracle in 28:15–16 evokes the constellation of Hananiah's first speech in 28:2–4 as well as 28:11 when it refers to "all the people." The accusation at the end of 28:15 condemns Hananiah for making the people trust in a lie. The message to which this accusation refers could, perhaps, be interpreted only in light of the explanation of the symbolic act in 28:11, but it makes more sense in light of the more extended speech of 28:2–4 or the combination of the two speeches. The messenger formula introducing accusation #1 is followed by the motivation that often appears as part of the concluding characterization. In these verses, it further explicates the accusation by providing the rationale for YHWH's action.

SALVATION ORACLES

The basic components of a salvation oracle, also called an oracle of deliverance, are not all that different from a judgment oracle. The major exception is, of course, that the salvation oracle provides comfort rather than judgment. Also, the characteristic markers of the transition points differ from one another. In contrast to the judgment oracle, where "therefore" serves as a key marker that the judgment is about to follow, the salvation oracle is likely to contain the phrase "fear not." Such is the case in the narrated oracle in Isaiah 7:1–7, when YHWH tells Isaiah to speak to King Ahaz of Judah and say, "Take heed, be quiet, *do not fear*, and do not let your heart be faint because of these two smoldering stumps of firebrands" (7:4).

Structural similarities between the judgment oracle and the salvation oracle are also strong. Like the judgment oracle, the salvation oracle indicates the situation and usually has some kind of concluding characterization. In between, one typically finds the pronouncement of salvation or deliverance. These three elements parallel elements two, three, and four in the outline of the judgment oracle. In the prophetic writings, oracles of salvation are considerably fewer in number than oracles of judgment. Nevertheless they can play an important role in understanding prophetic forms and the role of the prophet in the cult. One example may suffice, especially given its significance in Jeremiah 28 for understanding the dynamic between Jeremiah and Hananiah in the judgment oracle in 28:12–17 discussed above. This chapter, portraying the confrontation between Hananiah and Jeremiah, begins with a salvation oracle delivered by Hananiah (28:2–4).

Chart 18: Jeremiah 28:1–4

Narrative Transition:	¹In that same year, at the beginning of the reign of King Zedekiah of Judah, in the fifth month of the fourth year, the prophet Hananiah son of Azzur, from Gibeon, spoke to me in the house of the LORD, in the presence of the priests and all the people, saying,
Messenger Formula:	²"Thus says the LORD of hosts, the God of Israel:
Pronouncement of Deliverance:	I have broken the yoke of the king of Babylon. ³Within two years I will bring back to this place all the vessels of the LORD's house, which King Nebuchadnezzar of Babylon took away from this place and carried to Babylon. ⁴I will also bring back to this place King Jeconiah son of Jehoiakim of Judah, and all the exiles from Judah who went to Babylon,
Concluding Characterization:	says the LORD, for I will break the yoke of the king of Babylon."

In this oracle, shown in chart 18, the narrative transition sets the stage by dating the encounter to the fourth year of Zedekiah's reign, introducing Hananiah the prophet, and locating the speech in the temple. What makes this introduction a transition, though, is that it also refers back to "that same year," a reference back to the previous date formula in 27:1. This previous episode recounted the symbolic action of Jeremiah, who was commanded by YHWH to wear a wooden yoke around his neck (27:2). This cross reference in 28:1 thus contextualizes the date of the encounter that follows; it also helps to explain the language of Hananiah's speech. Since Jeremiah had already put on a wooden yoke in chapter 27 to symbolize God's decision to place Judah and other nations under the yoke of Babylon's power, it is no accident that Hananiah begins his pronouncement of deliverance with the statement that YHWH has broken the yoke of Babylon's king. This pronouncement explicates the meaning of that statement by stating that within two years the temple utensils will be returned, the king will be restored to Judah, and the exiles sent to Babylon in 597 BCE will return to Jerusalem.

In other words, while Jeremiah conveyed a message of judgment with the symbolic action of the yoke, Hananiah counters that message with a salvation oracle. Hananiah's salvation oracle begins with a messenger formula ("Thus says YHWH"), and the prophet speaks in the divine first person. Both of these elements emphasize Hananiah's claim to speak under YHWH's authority. Short of calling him by name, Hananiah could not have made it any clearer: he was claiming that YHWH had revoked Jeremiah's message. Both of these elements (Hananiah's speaking for YHWH and using Jeremiah's symbolic language) appear again in the concluding characterization, which provides an emphatic statement to close the oracle.

In a few short verses, the narrative will also present Hananiah's own symbolic action, removing the yoke from Jeremiah (28:10). It is these two acts of Hananiah, the salvation oracle falsely delivered in the name of YHWH and the removal of Jeremiah's yoke, that create the scene in which Jeremiah utters the judgment oracle in 28:12–17 (see the discussion of this judgment oracle above). Hence, Jeremiah 27–28 utilizes a significant number of characteristic prophetic forms, interrelated by language and content, in order to illustrate and heighten the tension between two prophetic figures, both claiming to speak for the same deity but delivering messages that contradict one another.

DISPUTATIONS

In this form, the prophet addresses charges made by the people against God or against the prophet. These charges can be spoken by the people, but more often the speaker (either YHWH or the prophet) states the charges and then counters them with arguments or with rhetorical questions. These elements can be clearly seen in Malachi 1:2–5, shown in chart 19.

These verses begin with a statement from YHWH pronouncing love for Israel. YHWH then quotes the dubious retort from the people, essentially demanding that YHWH prove this opening statement. In response, YHWH draws upon literary and contemporary realia to illustrate the thesis. YHWH alludes to the stories of Jacob and Esau from Genesis 25, where the twins vie for the love of Rachel and Isaac. YHWH, however, chooses to continue the

Chart 19: Malachi 1:2–5

Thesis:	[2]I have loved you, says the LORD.
Call for Proof:	But you say, "How have you loved us?"
Response:	Is not Esau Jacob's brother? says the LORD. Yet I have loved Jacob [3]but I have hated Esau; I have made his hill country a desolation and his heritage a desert for jackals. [4]If Edom says, "We are shattered but we will rebuild the ruins," the LORD of hosts says: They may build, but I will tear down, until they are called the wicked country, the people with whom the LORD is angry forever.
Final Affirmation:	[5]Your own eyes shall see this, and you shall say, "Great is the LORD beyond the borders of Israel!"

ancestral promise through Jacob (Gen. 28:13–14). Malachi 1:2–4 presupposes knowledge of this story by alluding to Jacob and Esau but assumes that the reader knows the descendants of these two characters are the people of Israel and Edom. Further, the speech assumes that the reader knows Israel is the name used for YHWH's people in Judah during the Persian period.

YHWH does not tell the story or state the connection between Esau and Edom or between Jacob, Israel, and Judah. Instead, YHWH assumes that the reader knows these relationships. YHWH then quotes Edom in order to emphasize that Edom's punishment will not be removed. The speech from Edom *assumes* that they are experiencing trouble politically ("We are shattered"). Scholars typically associate this statement with Edom's problems with attacks from the Nabateans in the fifth century BCE. The logic here is clear. Israel's political status is better than the political status of Edom, thereby demonstrating how YHWH's election of Jacob/Israel/Judah has benefited them. Thus YHWH's example combines literary and sociopolitical assumptions to prove the original claim that YHWH loves Jacob.

TRIAL SPEECHES

The trial speech, also called the *rîb*, contains three recurring elements: a summons to listen, trial speeches by the prosecution and/or the defense, and a verdict (most commonly in the form of a declaration of guilt) where the sentence is handed down. It is unusual to find all three elements together. Often, some of these elements can appear by themselves, especially when YHWH speaks accusations as though addressing a court (e.g., Isa. 50:1–3).

The summons may contain a call to listen or a call to be a witness to the proceedings that follow. The heavens and earth are often named as witnesses, but other groups may be named as well. The trial typically unfolds in a rather abbreviated fashion, using speeches by the prosecutor (YHWH). The prosecutor's speech may question the accused, but these rhetorical questions seldom leave any doubt about how the prosecutor believes the accused should respond. Most commonly the prosecutor's speech also constitutes the accusation.

In the declaration of guilt, one does not often find a clear delineation between the prosecutor and the judge in the constellation of characters. Unlike modern courtroom settings, biblical trial speeches often presume that YHWH is both the prosecuting attorney and the judge pronouncing the verdict. Whether this function reflects ancient juridical practices or whether these roles are blended for theological reasons is uncertain, but these roles typically blend together in biblical trial speeches.

Chart 20: Micah 6:9–16

Summons:	[9]The voice of the Lord cries to the city (it is sound wisdom to fear your name): Hear, O tribe and assembly of the city!
Indictment Speech with Accusations:	[10]Can I forget the treasures of wickedness in the house of the wicked, and the scant measure that is accursed? [11]Can I tolerate wicked scales and a bag of dishonest weights? [12]Your wealthy are full of violence; your inhabitants speak lies, with tongues of deceit in their mouths.
Verdict:	[13]Therefore I have begun to strike you down, making you desolate because of your sins. [14]You shall eat, but not be satisfied, and there shall be a gnawing hunger within you; you shall put away, but not save, and what you save, I will hand over to the sword. [15]You shall sow, but not reap; you shall tread olives, but not anoint yourselves with oil; you shall tread grapes, but not drink wine.
Summation of Accusation and Verdict:	[16]For you have kept the statutes of Omri and all the works of the house of Ahab, and you have followed their counsels. Therefore I will make you a desolation, and your inhabitants an object of hissing; so you shall bear the scorn of my people.

Micah 6:9–16 in chart 20 illustrates the trial speech quite clearly, incorporating the three constituent elements (summons, accusation, verdict) as well as a concluding summary.

The summons proper appears in Micah 6:9b, where it addresses the defendant with a call to listen. The prosecutor speaks the indictment with a series of rhetorical questions framed to convince those listening that YHWH has no choice but to act. The questions ask whether YHWH can ignore a series of dishonest actions on Judah's part. No one can doubt that the answer to these questions would be no. These questions give way to direct accusations as the city is accused of violence and deceit in 6:12.

Having expressed the charges, YHWH moves immediately to the verdict. YHWH announces a punishment that involves famine and military oppression (6:13–15). These images leading to desolation imply a process of increasing depravity. YHWH announces the beginning of the punishment ("I have *begun* to strike you down") as a situation in which constant hunger is the norm (6:14a). This period of hunger, according to 6:14b, will be followed by a period of military oppression ("I will hand over to the sword"). The three remaining punishments should be understood poetically to indicate a dramatic breakdown of the normal agricultural process (no grain, olive oil, or wine). The disruption in fertility results from God's action.

The accusation and the verdict are summarized to conclude the trial in 6:16. Accusations that the country has followed the paths of Omri and Ahab pick up the same motif with which Micah began, namely, that judgment against Judah happens because they have begun to behave like the northern kingdom, worshiping deities other than YHWH (see Mic. 1:5–7, 8–9). Investigation of these two kings in particular sheds further light (see chap. 3: "Selecting Key Words"). Not only are Omri and Ahab northern kings from the same dynasty, but in the books of 1 and 2 Kings they (especially Ahab) represent the worst kings of the northern kingdom. Thus for YHWH to accuse Judah of acting like Ahab and Omri draws upon a very powerful negative symbol of a king who worships Baal rather than YHWH, kills prophets, and terrorizes his own people through his malfeasance. This trial speech, like most examples of the genre, utilizes very pointed rhetoric to convey its accusations.

SYMBOLIC-ACT REPORT

Formally, the symbolic-act report involves three elements: (1) the command to perform a particular action; (2) a report of the performance of said command; and (3) an interpretation of the symbolic act. All four books of the Latter Prophets contain these reports, but they are particularly prominent and vivid in Ezekiel.

Hosea 1:2–9 begins with the report of a symbolic act whose execution is recounted in four parts, as shown in chart 21. This passage contains several features important for understanding the report of a symbolic action. First, the initial symbolic act lays the groundwork for three subsequent accounts. Second, all four accounts are interrelated. Third, apart from the first example, the report component focuses less upon recounting that the command was performed than it does on transitioning to the next symbolic act (i.e., the report of a new child). Fourth, the interpretation relates differently to the symbol in the first two and the last two actions. In the first two actions, the interpretation draws an analogy to the symbol. In 1:2, the land is compared to a prostitute, while the relationship between the prophet and the prostitute is compared to the relationship of YHWH to the land. Similarly, the first son's name, Jezreel, draws an analogy to the place where the previous dynasty ended in order to pronounce judgment against the current dynasty and the kingdom of Israel. By contrast, with the third and fourth commands, the name itself pronounces the judgment since Lo-ruhamah means "not pitied" and Lo-ammi means "not my people." Fifth, the brevity with which these overlapping symbolic act reports are conveyed to the reader masks the fact that the birth of the three children would, at a

Chart 21: Hosea 1:2–9

Command #1:	[2]When the LORD first spoke through Hosea, the LORD said to Hosea,
	"Go, take for yourself a wife of whoredom and have children of whoredom,
Interpretation #1:	for the land commits great whoredom by forsaking the LORD."
Report #1:	[3]So he went and took Gomer daughter of Diblaim, and she conceived and bore him a son.
Command #2:	[4]And the LORD said to him, "Name him Jezreel;
Interpretation #2:	for in a little while I will punish the house of Jehu for the blood of Jezreel, and I will put an end to the kingdom of the house of Israel. [5]On that day I will break the bow of Israel in the valley of Jezreel."
Report #2:	[6]She conceived again and bore a daughter. Then the LORD said to him,
Command #3:	"Name her Lo-ruhamah,
Interpretation #3:	for I will no longer have pity on the house of Israel or forgive them. [7]But I will have pity on the house of Judah, and I will save them by the LORD their God; I will not save them by bow, or by sword, or by war, or by horses, or by horsemen."
Report #3:	[8]When she had weaned Lo-ruhamah, she conceived and bore a son.
Command #4:	[9]Then the LORD said, "Name him Lo-ammi,
Interpretation #4:	for you are not my people and I am not your God."

minimum, take close to three years to occur. This point once again serves as a reminder that prophetic units, even when they purport to be biographical in nature, have been shaped for theological reasons. The message, not the messenger, is the central focus.

Ezekiel 4–5 relates a number of symbolic acts designed to portray YHWH's judgment against Jerusalem, Judah, and Israel. These chapters contain, in sequence, commands to the prophet to do the following: to use a brick to represent the city (4:1–3); to lie first on one side and then on the other to represent the days of punishment for Israel and Judah (4:4–8); to eat fixed measures of food cooked over manure to portray the eating of unclean bread in clean land (4:9–15); and to cut his hair into thirds to represent the fate of the people of Jerusalem (5:1–6). The cumulative effect of these symbolic acts and their interpretations conveys the dramatic sense of impending danger for YHWH's people. Moreover, the symbolic acts make clear to the reader that the calamities faced by YHWH's people should be understood as judgment from YHWH.

These claims, ironically, function as claims of faith. Judah experienced two exiles (597 and 587 BCE), the overthrow of two kings, and the devastating destruction of the temple in Jerusalem. It would have been easy for those exiled to Babylon to have abandoned the worship of YHWH and their identity. Instead, the evidence suggests that the words of prophets like Ezekiel helped to keep the exiled community together by interpreting their suffering as punishment from YHWH, and consequently by interpreting their survival as hope for a future in which YHWH would one day bring them back.

A third illustration of the role that symbolic action reports play in the message of prophetic writings can be illustrated briefly, yet importantly, in Jeremiah 27:2; 28:10–11. We already noted above the close association of Jeremiah 28 with Jeremiah 27, despite the fact that each of these chapters begins with its own superscription (27:1; 28:1) and uses a significant variety of distinct forms, even while linking the message of the two chapters (including superscriptions, the judgment oracle, salvation oracle, and symbolic-action report).

In fact, Jeremiah 27:2 opens these chapters with a symbolic-action report in which Jeremiah is commanded to put a wooden yoke around his neck. In this instance, the command is not followed by a report that the action was carried out by the prophet. Nevertheless, the remainder of chapter 27 essentially consists of commentary about the implications of this symbolic action. Further, the superscription in 28:1 refers back to the events of 27:1–2, and 28:10–11 includes the report of Hananiah's own symbolic act when he removed the yoke from Jeremiah and broke it in front of the people.

Hananiah's action thus attempts to annul the message of judgment implicit in the actions of Jeremiah's wearing of the yoke. Hananiah's action is consistent with the salvation oracle he delivers in 28:2–4, but when Jeremiah receives word from YHWH that Hananiah has acted on his own, even though he claimed to be acting on YHWH's behalf, the resulting judgment oracle and its narrative frame (28:12–17) portray Jeremiah as the genuine prophet and Hananiah as a deceiver. This confrontation between two prophets, both claiming to speak on YHWH's behalf and both drawing upon genuine prophetic forms and formulas, demonstrates that even in biblical times, theological battles existed over who spoke genuinely on God's behalf.

VISION REPORTS

The vision report is, in many ways, quite similar to the symbolic-act report. Instead of a command to perform an act, though, the prophet is shown an object by YHWH. The act of seeing this object is recounted to the reader, sometimes in a visionary formula (e.g., "YHWH showed me . . .") or with a series of questions (e.g., "what do you see?"). Typically, the implications of the vision are then explained for the benefit of the reader. In two cases, a series of interrelated vision reports serves as the basis for a major section of a prophetic writing. The five increasingly threatening visions of Amos (7:1–3, 4–6, 7–9; 8:1–3; 9:1–4) provide the foundational material around which Amos 7–9 is structured. Similarly, Zechariah 1:8–6:15 conveys the core message of Zechariah 1–8 through a series of eight vision reports and the commentary associated with them. Vision reports also appear in other prophetic writings. Consider the two vision reports near the beginning of Jeremiah (1:11–12, 13–14), as shown in chart 22. Both vision reports begin with questions from YHWH to the prophet.

In both visions, the items seen by the prophet appear relatively innocuous. In the first instance, the item seen becomes a vehicle for a pun to convey the impression that YHWH is watching. The word "almond" (šāqēd) plays off the participial form of "watch over" (šōqēd). The same thing happens in the second vision, although the pun is more oblique than in the first case, since the root from which the word "boiling" comes (nāpaḥ) rhymes with the verb "break out" (pātaḥ). Thus the items in the two visions have no theological significance in and of themselves but merely serve as vehicles for puns to deliver a very somber message.

Chart 22: Jeremiah 1:11–14

Question 1:	[11]The word of the LORD came to me, saying, "Jeremiah, what do you see?"
Vision 1:	And I said, "I see a branch of an *almond* tree (šāqēd)."
Interpretation:	[12]Then the LORD said to me, "You have seen well, for I am *watching over* (šōqēd) my word to perform it."
Question 2:	[13]The word of the LORD came to me a second time, saying, "What do you see?"
Vision 2:	And I said, "I see a *boiling* (nāpûaḥ) pot, tilted away from the *north* (ṣāpônāh)."
Interpretation:	[14]Then the LORD said to me: Out of the *north* (ṣāpôn) disaster shall *break out* (tippātaḥ) on all the inhabitants of the land. [15]For now I am calling all the tribes of the kingdoms of the north, says the LORD; and they shall come and all of them shall set their thrones at the entrance of the gates of Jerusalem, against all its surrounding walls and against all the cities of Judah.

PROMISES

As a rule, prophetic writings contain much more material concerning judgment and confrontation of YHWH's people than messages of hope and deliverance. Nevertheless, it has long been noted that most of the prophetic writings have been edited with an eye toward making sure that the writing closes with a message of hope. Scholars in the twentieth century established that many of these hopeful passages were later additions to the writings, especially with early collections such as Hosea, Amos, Micah, and Zephaniah. The reasons for considering these promises to be later additions, however, had less to do with their role as promises than it did with the sense that the promises were directed toward people who had already experienced the destruction of Jerusalem and Judah, despite the fact that the prophetic figure for whom the book was named was dated before the destruction. In later writings, such as Joel and Haggai, the promises seem to function as a more integral part of the entire book, even if (as in the case of Joel) scholars debate whether Joel constitutes a single composition or developed in stages. Nevertheless, the promises and prophetic writings are not all cut from the same cloth. Promises can function within calls to repentance, or as eschatological hope for a change to the current situation. Both kinds of promises, however, can manifest differently in their literary context.

Promises within Calls to Repentance

If one considers the role of promises in calls to repentance (e.g., Hos. 14:1–8; and Joel 2:18–27, following the call to repentance in 2:12–17), one can see that what they promise is contingent upon the people's responding to the call to repent. In neither case, however, does the narrator report that the people actually do repent, leaving the reader to determine whether or not the promise has been actualized or left open. The final chapter of Hosea begins with a call to repent (14:1) followed by the introduction of the speech that the people are to speak (14:2–3). The promise comes from YHWH in 14:5–7, but the admonition in 14:8 implies that YHWH still waits for the people of Ephraim (i.e., the northern kingdom) to respond.

Joel 2:18–27 is even more ambiguous. The purpose of this promise is designed to reverse the threats, natural and military, to the land described in Joel 1. The fact that a narrated response is lacking, however, makes it uncertain whether to treat YHWH's speech as a response to the repentance or as a promise *if* the people repent. The NRSV translators treat the speech as the former and use the past tense. By contrast, the NIV considers the speech from YHWH as a promise and translates the speech using the future tense.

Eschatological and Protoapocalyptic Promises

In addition to promises that function as part of calls to repentance, many prophetic writings end with eschatological promises that offer hope for a changed world, a world where a restored Jerusalem represents a place of peace, a place of agricultural fertility, and even a place of worship for the nations. Many, but not all, of these promises appear at the end of prophetic writings, thereby reflecting a theological conviction that individual prophetic writings should end with words of promise. This practice seems to have begun in the exilic period and continued as most of the writings were shaped into their final form in the postexilic period.

Amos 9:11–15 offers a revealing case in point, as illustrated in chart 23. Not only does this passage offer a word of hope that is otherwise absent from Amos, but the message of hope for restoration it contains reflects two very different portraits of what that restoration looks like. On the one hand, portions of this passage describe the future in terms of a renewal of the past; on the other hand, the remaining portions depict a verdant future, the likes of which have never been seen.

The promises in most of this passage focus upon restoring what has been lost to Jerusalem: its king, its kingdom, its cities, and the normal fertility of its land. Amos 9:11–12 portrays the future in terms of the idealized kingdom. Unlike most of Amos, however, where the message of judgment was directed against the northern kingdom, 9:11–12 presumes that Judah, not Israel, stands in need of restoration. This passage presumes that the "fallen booth of David" will be rebuilt (9:11), a statement that makes sense only after Jerusalem has been destroyed. Further, this restoration will lead to the reestablishment of the Davidic kingdom (9:12). Before that can happen, however, cities must be rebuilt, the land must yield its produce again (9:14), and exiles must return (9:15). Needless to say, these promises are delivered as words of hope because

Chart 23: Amos 9:11–15

[11]On that day I will raise up the booth of David that is fallen, and repair its breaches, and raise up its ruins, and rebuild it as in the days of old; [12]in order that they may possess the remnant of Edom and all the nations who are called by my name, says the LORD who does this.

> [13]The time is surely coming, says the LORD, when the one who plows shall overtake the one who reaps, and the treader of grapes the one who sows the seed; the mountains shall drip sweet wine, and all the hills shall flow with it.

[14]I will restore the fortunes of my people Israel, and they shall rebuild the ruined cities and inhabit them; they shall plant vineyards and drink their wine, and they shall make gardens and eat their fruit. [15]I will plant them upon their land, and they shall never again be plucked up out of the land that I have given them, says the LORD your God.

the situation is not what people currently experience. This promise, then, offers hope in the aftermath of Jerusalem's disruption and the exile of much of its population. These verses paint the ideal future in terms of the ideal past.

By contrast, Amos 9:13 portrays the agricultural bounty in grandiose terms, the likes of which never existed in the ancient world. This word of hope depicts harvests so huge that the work of bringing in the crops will still be going on when it is time to till the soil and plant the fields once again. This verse envisions an abundance of wine flowing from the mountains. The promise of 9:13 makes the promise of 9:14 rather anticlimactic. If the land in the mountains were producing crops as described in 9:13, then the promise of replanting vines and making gardens would hardly seem necessary. The fact that 9:13b cites Joel 3:18 (MT 4:18), whose vision of the abundant future fits more consistently with its context in Joel, suggests that this grander vision was inserted into Amos 9 with an eye toward linking the two writings at a later time.

Other promise texts, for example, Isaiah 66 and Zechariah 14, appear to be composite collections of small thematic units. Zechariah 14 contains a series of promises depicting the day of YHWH as a day of promise for Jerusalem that will restore the city's role as the center of the world and the place where all the nations will come to worship YHWH. Similarly, Isaiah 66 portrays Zion as a place of rejoicing, where YHWH will defeat the nations and rule over a purified earth. Both Isaiah 66 and Zechariah 14 presume a functioning temple. By comparison, Ezekiel 40–48 anticipates the rebuilding of the temple, albeit one quite different from the one actually built, and a restoration of the cultic apparatus, as well as a reestablishment of the tribal system when the land is restored. While these promises explore some similar themes, their goals and focus reflect different political and theological agendas for the future.

Messianic Promises

When they begin studying prophetic literature seriously, most Christian students are surprised to learn that prophetic literature does not focus primarily upon messianic predictions. Unfortunately, many churches and religious traditions have perpetuated a view that the primary purpose of the prophets was to foretell the coming of the Messiah. This misperception derives from many influences, but space does not allow a full exploration.

The prophets, in their original context, were not primarily oriented toward predicting the coming Messiah. Nevertheless, one does periodically find prophetic texts that tie into messianic themes. Caution must be exercised, however; the serious reader needs to understand these messianic themes in their Old Testament context before moving on to the question of how these texts have been appropriated by New Testament writers or by later Christian interpreters. This later reception history has seen something significant in these texts that drew the attention of Christian interpreters to see parallels to the life of Jesus, but these parallels rarely relate directly to the immediate Old Testament context in which these promises appear.

In the Old Testament, the term "messiah" means "anointed one" and relates primarily to royal figures. Kings were conceived as God's representatives on earth. To convey this concept, some texts even refer to the king as the son of God (e.g., Ps. 2:7). A king functions primarily as the head of the political and military apparatus of the country. In this respect, it is important to remember that most of the prophetic collections reflect a strong Jerusalemite ideology, meaning that any royal figure would be associated with the Davidic dynasty, whether past, present, or future. Several promises of restoration in the prophetic corpus include a hope that Davidic rule will once again be established in Jerusalem. This hope takes several forms, depending upon how a given text envisions the political role of king in relation to Judah.

Deutero-Isaiah, for example, downplays the identity of the king as a descendant of David, opting instead to portray Cyrus, king of Persia, as YHWH's anointed. This idea is made explicit in Isaiah 44:28–45:1, where YHWH claims that it is YHWH

> 44:28who says of Cyrus, "He is my shepherd, and he shall carry out all my purpose"; and who says of Jerusalem, "It shall be rebuilt," and of the temple, "Your foundation shall be laid." 45:1Thus says the LORD to his anointed, to Cyrus, whose right hand I have grasped to subdue nations before him and strip kings of their robes, to open doors before him—and the gates shall not be closed.

When this passage is placed against the three traditional elements of Zion theology, its radical message becomes even clearer. Texts steeped in traditional Zion theology regularly highlight three motifs: YHWH's selection of Jerusalem as the place to dwell, YHWH's choice of David and David's descendants to rule for YHWH in Jerusalem, and YHWH's decision to protect Jerusalem from the nations. These verses in Isaiah 44–45 focus on precisely the same themes, with the exception that Cyrus, king of Persia, has replaced David as YHWH's representative and protector of Jerusalem.

Micah 5:2, by contrast, hopes for a ruler of Jerusalem who, like David of old, comes from Bethlehem of Judah, a village only five miles south of Jerusalem, who will lead the people home and restore peace. Haggai 2:23 is even more specific in portraying Zerubbabel, the grandson of Jehoiachin (the last legitimate king of Judah, who was taken into exile in the first deportation of 597), as YHWH's servant and chosen one to rule on YHWH's behalf. Haggai connects Zerubbabel with an overthrow of the nations (see 2:21–22). Haggai's hopes for this descendant of David, however, never came to fruition. This does not mean, however, that the hope for a new Davidic king died with him.

Rather, hopes for the restoration of a Davidic monarch remained alive, at least in some circles. Such hopes can be seen in a text written considerably later, Zechariah 9:9–10, but in this text the king returns in peace (riding on a donkey), but after the description of YHWH clearing the land of foreign threats, essentially forming a shield around Jerusalem (note the movement of YHWH's cleansing of the land from north to south, moving from Syria, to Phoenicia, to Philistia in Zech. 9:1–10).

Given the political nature of many of these messianic promises, it is no wonder that Jesus spends a good deal of time clarifying that his role as Messiah is not defined by these political expectations. Jesus does not portray himself as a new David, out to retake Jerusalem from foreign occupying armies. Jesus understands the kingdom of God quite differently.

CONCLUDING OBSERVATIONS

The selection of prophetic forms discussed above is neither exhaustive nor determinative. Numerous other genres could be explored here as well, and students are advised to consult critical commentaries for the forms used in various prophetic texts. When commentators refer to these forms, it is usually because they represent patterns of linguistic formulations and logic that recur elsewhere in Old Testament prophetic literature. These patterns would include, among others, calls to repent (e.g., Isa. 14; Joel 1–2; Zech. 1:2–6); call narratives (Isa. 6; Jer. 1; Ezek. 1–2; Jonah 1:2; 3:2–3); oracles against the nations (Isa. 13–23; Jer. 46–51; Ezek. 25–32; Amos 1–2); and woe oracles (five of which appear in Hab. 2:6–19 and six of which appear in Isa. 5:8–22), to name but a few. Recognition of the patterns reflected in these forms offers significant insight into the logic of texts, and often their placement within the prophetic writings.

It should be emphatically reiterated, however, that these patterns are not molds into which prophetic speech is poured. Remember the two modern illustrations provided at the beginning of this chapter: the phrases "Dearly beloved" and "Hi, I'm not here right now." If the speaker begins, "Dearly beloved," but continues, "we are gathered here to bury the fool," a reader would quickly intuit that the setting is much more likely to be a toast at a bachelor party than the actual beginning of a wedding. Or consider the socio-historical implications of the voice mail greeting: "Hi, I'm not here right now." If someone heard a speaker say this line in the 1940s, the sanity of the speaker might very well have been questioned, because the technology and applications that gave rise to the repetition of this phrase did not yet exist.

The same thing can happen with Old Testament forms. Often the creative departure from an expected pattern is as indicative of the prophetic speech as the pattern itself. For example, Amos 4:4 likely draws upon a well-known call to worship, but it is not a call to worship. Amos 4:4 does not say, "Come to Bethel and worship." Rather, it turns that form upon its ear when it says instead, "Come to Bethel—and sin." These patterns are helpful, but one must treat each example carefully, noting where it corresponds to similar texts drawing upon a given pattern and where it differs from them.

Further, sometimes forms point to certain historical presumptions that help to illuminate a particular text. Examples of this were seen in the introduction of Cyrus as the anointed one in Isaiah 45:1 and in the promises to restore Jerusalem (e.g., Amos 9:11–15) that would make little sense if they did not presume Jerusalem had already been destroyed. These comparisons of patterns and the implications of forms are part of what makes the interpretation of biblical texts an art rather than a science.

5

Analyzing a Unit's Relationship
to the Context

CONTEXTUAL CLUES

In addition to the careful reading of each poetic line, one should also evaluate how poetic lines relate to the immediate and larger contexts. Typically, poetic lines are paired with other poetic lines to make verses, and these verses are related in some way to the surrounding context. Determining that relationship frequently involves some level of debate; so beginning students are particularly encouraged at this point to consult multiple commentaries before landing too quickly upon one particular interpretation. These debates aside, the task of interpreting a poetic unit in light of its context involves at least five different aspects: placement of logia, syntactical connectors, thematic cohesion, controlling metaphors, and literary horizon. Together these elements may also suggest how to understand the components of a prophetic book through the growth of smaller compositions and collections. As with other tasks in the interpretive process, these aspects do not represent a linear sequence of tasks to perform but issues to be evaluated for the light they shed upon the text in conjunction with other elements. The art of interpretation involves consideration of these aspects, but they do not function in isolation from one another or from the tasks described in chapters 1–4.

Placement of Logia

In 1979 Walter Zimmerli penned an article that crystallized an important understanding regarding how prophetic materials were gathered into the collections that we now have. Specifically, Zimmerli noted that almost all prophetic collections begin with judgment sayings against Israel or Judah.[1]

Conversely, most of the prophetic writings end with some kind of eschatological promise or collection of oracles against the nations. This observation has important implications, since it suggests that the process of arrangement of prophetic materials has more to do with theological concerns than with biographical reportage.

Consider, for example, the book of Ezekiel, where two overlapping schema dominate the structural movement of the book. First, Ezekiel exhibits a series of chronological superscriptions that, unlike the book of Jeremiah, appear in largely chronological order covering more than a twenty-year time frame. Second, Ezekiel clearly exhibits the threefold eschatological movements noted by Zimmerli. The first half of the book contains largely messages of judgment (chaps. 1–24). The middle (chaps. 25–32) contain oracles against foreign nations. The concluding chapters contain two sections of promise that show an increasingly eschatological orientation (chaps. 33–39 and 40–48). Careful analysis of all the speech units in Ezekiel, however, strongly suggests that these date formulas superimpose a chronological sequence on the book that is not consistent with the dates of the individual oracles contained between these chronological introductions. In other words, the thematic groupings of judgment, oracles against the nations, and promise are more consistent than the chronological frame of the dated sayings. Put another way, it is hardly likely that prophets were trained to speak judgment as young men and pronounce promises when they got older. More likely, the movement from judgment to promise, so evident in many of the prophetic writings, has to do with the collection and compilation of the sayings and smaller collections.

Further, sections within prophetic books often suggest that smaller collections have been joined together editorially. For example, Zechariah 1–6 contains a series of eight vision reports and commentary on those reports, while Zechariah 7–8 groups together numerous short sayings, where a new introductory formula begins every few verses. The grouping of the reports in Zechariah 1–6 presents a series of visions as a sequence of prophetic encounters (presumably on a single night), some of which presume the reader knows the preceding encounters. By contrast, the coherence of the logia in Zechariah 7–8 derives more from grouping units that display common themes than from a single composition. The arrangement of short summaries and prophetic pronouncements often reflects thematic variations conjoined for theological and didactic reasons. One does not necessarily expect to find a sustained argument connecting such units. That being said, this section opens with a lengthy question by a delegation of leaders from Bethel to the priests and prophets in Jerusalem (7:2–3). These questions are not answered until 8:18, which means that the question and response (7:1–3; 8:18) now frame the sayings, suggesting that the collection of sayings in between should be understood as knowledge necessary to understand the response of Zechariah to those questions.

Syntactical Connectors

This task has already been discussed (in chap. 2), but it is mentioned here again because the wide variety of connective elements within prophetic books can function on many levels. As noted in the discussion of Joel 2:18, one connector can functionally join two sentences, but it can also mark a significant turning point in the collective understanding of the writing in which it appears. In the case of Joel 2:18, the Hebrew syntax extends the action of 2:12–17 (albeit in a way that is ambiguous), but the verse also marks a major turning point in the book, both thematically and stylistically. Thematically, the promise language that begins in 2:18 continues through the end of Joel, though several units comprise those promises. Stylistically, the prophet has been the speaker throughout most of Joel 1:2–2:17, but after 2:18 YHWH speaks in the first person.

Similar transition points can be seen in other writings. For example, the units in Amos 1–2 are easily recognizable by the recurring refrain, "for three transgressions and for four," which appears eight times (1:3, 6, 9, 11, 13; 2:1, 4, 6), with the first six naming foreign entities. The final oracles, however, announce YHWH's judgment against Judah and then Israel. By contrast, Amos 3–6 contains a collection of short sayings of diverse origins, but these sayings are arranged in four groups, the first three beginning with "hear this word" (3:1; 4:1; 5:1) while the fourth group begins like a funeral dirge: "woe to . . ." (6:1). In a certain sense, this change from the call to attention ("Hear this word") to a woe oracle, with its funerary overtones, subtly suggests a shift to an even more pessimistic outlook.

Another illustration can be found in Habakkuk 1:5, where the opening word ("behold") suggests a new unit, and the divine speaker marks a change from the prophetic speaker of 1:2–4. The attentive reader will intuit that the divine speech in 1:5–11 represents YHWH's response to the question "how long?" that began in 1:2, despite the fact that the divine speech addresses a group (the plural imperatives), while the prophet had prayed directly to YHWH. The prayer and the response thus were not likely a single composition but represent an editor's decision to use the oracle about YHWH's use of Babylon to punish Judah (1:5–11) as a response to the prophet's cry for justice. The presence of these transition points is almost universally recognized by commentators, but it falls to the individual interpreters to explain their significance in the context. These explanations may vary widely.

Finally, introductory formulas and other devices can provide editorial clues regarding the intention of those who added a text. For example, the formula "on that day" has long been recognized among scholars as a signal frequently used by scribes to expand an existing text with new material, though not every instance of the phrase can be assumed as secondary. The chronological implications of the phrase for readers of such passages are less commonly acknowledged and explored. The use of the demonstrative pronoun ("that") assumes an antecedent, which usually refers to divine action or divinely initiated action in the future. The phrase "on that day" introduces new actions or expanded consequences by situating them in the same time frame as the previous material. For example, consider Isaiah 7:17–25. This passage begins with a statement that the king of Assyria will attack YHWH's people. Four subsequent occurrences of "on that day" (7:18, 20, 21, 23) expand the implications agriculturally and militarily. Scholars may debate the extent to which these short units represent later perspectives, but the rhetorical effect should not be missed. These four formulas portray all of the action as a consequence of the punishment announced in 7:17.

Thematic Cohesion

Both on the level of individual units and the larger sections within prophetic books, interpreters may detect degrees of coherence based on theme. For example, Isaiah 10 consists of a number of smaller sayings and speeches that deal, in various ways, with the anticipated demise of the Assyrian king. These smaller units deal with the issue from several perspectives. They may focus upon YHWH's confrontation with the king (10:12–19); they may mention the country by name (10:5–7); they may address a remnant of Israel who will survive the Assyrian onslaught (10:20–23). The internal linguistic cohesion within these smaller units appears stronger than the cohesion between the units. Nevertheless, the cumulative effect of this grouping of anti-Assyria sayings also needs to be considered when interpreting the smaller units. The presence of multiple units exploring a common theme creates a particular emphasis in the collection.

Controlling Metaphors and Catchwords

Similar to the grouping of sayings and speeches sharing similar themes, larger passages may consist of collections of sayings grouped together because they share metaphors, catchwords, or other images with neighboring speeches in the context. For example, consider Ezekiel 12:21–13:23. Ezekiel 12:21–28 deals with YHWH's judgment on the false prophets. Ezekiel 13:1 contains a new introductory speech, but internal signs do not indicate it was delivered at the same time as 12:21–28. However, even though 13:1 introduces a new speech, it also deals with the problem of prophets who speak their own words and not YHWH's words. Hence Ezekiel 12:24 talks about "false visions" and "flattering divinations" that do not come true.

These visions cause skepticism among the people that any vision will come true. This speech is delivered to the "house of Israel." The speech in 13:1–16 begins with similar words when it announces YHWH's judgment against false prophets who "envision" nothing but say they do (13:3) and who see a false "vision" and "lying divination" (13:7). Following condemnation of the male prophets in this unit, 13:17–23 takes on the female prophets who also mislead the people by their lies and pronounce "false visions" and "divination" (13:23). The combination of male and female prophets who deliberately mislead people about the source of their message thus combines several units and underscores Ezekiel's polemic against (false) prophets earning their living by proclaiming their own message. The combination of these units links them by catchwords ("false visions" and "divination"), some of which may have been implanted by editors to stress the connections between the accounts that they place together. The effect is cumulative and leaves the impression of a social situation that is out of control. No one can trust the words of those who claim to speak for God.

Literary Horizon

Recent studies in prophetic literature have demonstrated that, not infrequently, one should consider the literary horizon for which a prophetic text was composed or compiled. These studies have argued that the shaping of prophetic books sometimes requires transitional compositions, recapitulations, anticipations, or conclusions that draw upon text from other parts of the prophetic corpus.

The writing of Joel concludes with a series of statements in 3:18–20 (MT 4:18–20), including citations of other prophetic writings, whose purpose includes the reversal of judgment imagery from chapters 1–2 into images of promise. So, for example, the streambeds are dried up in 1:20, but they shall flow with water according to 3:18; the wine is cut off in 1:5 (see also 1:10, 12), but it will drip from the mountains in 3:18; the inhabitants of Judah and Jerusalem are threatened throughout chapters 1–2, but according to 3:20 (MT 4:20) Judah and Jerusalem will be continually inhabited. In this sense, the end of Joel appears to be designed intentionally to offer words of promise that reverse the situation of chapters 1–2.

Amos 8:4–14, which comes between the fourth and fifth vision reports, capitulates themes, phrases, and motifs from elsewhere in Amos. This placement before the final vision describing the destruction of Israel suggests that 8:4–14 plays the role of a kind of summation at a significant stage of the book's development. See further discussion below under the section entitled "The Growth of Collections."

Literary cross-references also appear in prophetic texts. For example, consider Ezekiel 43:1–4, a text that reverses the judgment described in Ezekiel 11:23 even as it refers to Ezekiel 1. In 43:2, the glory (*kābôd*) of YHWH returns from east of the city, thus reversing the departure of the glory (*kābôd*) of YHWH envisioned in 11:23. Ezekiel 43:3 also refers back to the book's initial vision when it refers to "the vision that I had seen by the river Chebar" (see 1:1). This cross-referencing underscores the message of hope that enables the book of Ezekiel to "anticipate" a vision of what the new temple would look like, according to those who transmitted the message of Ezekiel.

Further, several studies in the last decades have focused upon Isaiah 34–35 as a bridge text that deliberately connects themes and motifs from Isaiah 1–33 with those of (at least portions of) Isaiah 40–66. In some models, chapters 34–35 even serve this transitional function for more than one redactional layer of the developing corpus. These and other texts suggest that the compilation of prophetic books involved a scribal literary awareness beyond merely collecting the words of a prophetic figure of the past. Increasingly, these and other passages like them are being investigated for their literary function.

These examples only begin to treat the many ways that prophetic books convey meaning. More work remains to be done in this arena, as the compositional history of the prophetic books as books (i.e., as literary entities in their own right) continues to be explored. Earlier impressions of prophetic books as more or less random repositories of prophetic speeches have given way to the realization that the meaning of the scroll itself also represents an important arena of investigation.

THE GROWTH OF COLLECTIONS

The final form of some prophetic books may reflect the combination of two or more smaller collections that have been joined to one another at some point in time. Consider the four major sections of the book of Amos. Amos begins with a series of oracles against the nations that start with the same introductory refrain ("Thus says YHWH: For three transgressions of X and for four, I will not take it back") when the next section changes to a new country (1:3, 6, 9, 11, 13; 2:1, 4, 6). Each of these units lays out charges against an individual nation or people group that denounce certain actions for which the prophet holds the group accountable in the name of YHWH. Most of the specific details of violence mentioned in these units have been lost to time. While the new introductions separate the individual sections, the repeating refrain also provides a certain sense of cohesion as well that suggests they belong together.

The reason for this repetition becomes clear when one considers the location and the sequence of the oracles. Geographically, these nations surround Judah and Israel, so that divine judgment goes forth against all those countries whose borders touch upon Judah and Israel: Syria to the north (1:3–5), the Philistines to the southwest (1:6–8), the Phoenicians to the northwest (1:9–10), and the three peoples east of the Jordan: Edom (1:11–12), the Ammonites (1:13–15), and the Moabites (2:1–3). This sequence not only pronounces judgment against the surrounding nations; it also sets up the rhetorical climax, as the last two units use the same refrain to announce judgment upon Judah (2:4–5) and Israel (2:6–16). The effect of this larger unit thus creates a cumulative rhetorical impression that goes beyond the individual units. The larger unit encircles Israel by announcing judgment upon other nations surrounding Israel before climaxing with the longest and most surprising of the oracles: judgment against Israel itself.

The second section of Amos (chaps. 3–6) functions differently. The headings in 3:1, 4:1, 5:1, and 6:1 create the impression of new beginnings. The units that follow these headings do not have a refrain and have the character of short sayings or speech summaries that are only loosely related to the oracles around them. They have neither the inherent logic of a lengthy composition nor the rhetorical surprise at the end of the larger unit that would suggest that these smaller collections were intended as a single entity. Rather, to speak of a cumulative effect could only be done in the form of variations on a theme: Israel has abandoned its obligations to YHWH, and judgment is coming. The incessant drumbeat of this message reverberates throughout this section of Amos. While it contains some very memorable sayings for which Amos is well known (e.g., 4:6–11; 5:18–20, 21–24), one cannot detect a distinct literary development like that of a longer composition.

The third section of Amos (7:1–9:6) appears to reflect an underlying composition of five vision reports (7:1–3, 4–6, 7–9; 8:1–3; 9:1–4) that, like the opening unit, have both an individual design and a collective design as a group. At the same time, the collection appears to have been expanded in two places: the insertion of a prophetic narrative (7:10–17) after the third vision and a theological reflection on the book in 8:4–14 before the final vision report. Both of these expansions serve a significant literary function; but first, one needs to understand the individual vision reports and to appreciate the climactic movement of the five vision reports as a group.

The vision reports follow a pattern—or better, two patterns. The first and second vision reports appear more similar to one another than to the third and fourth. These repeating patterns create expectations, but the pattern then changes. The first two vision reports have the prophet seeing a devastating vision whose meaning leaves little doubt. In the first vision, the prophet sees a locust plague devouring the land. The prophet intercedes, and YHWH removes the judgment. In the second vision (7:4–6), the prophet sees a cosmic fire devouring the land; he again intercedes immediately, and YHWH takes back the judgment.

Visions three (7:7–9) and four (8:1–3) follow a different pattern. The prophet sees innocuous items that by themselves do not cause great distress (a lump of metal in 7:7 and a basket of summer fruit in 8:1). The prophet confirms that he sees these elements (7:8; 8:2), but does not intercede for the people as in the first two visions. The lump of metal serves as a sign that YHWH will never again pass over them. The basket of summer fruit becomes the subject of a pun since the summer fruit (Heb. qāyiṣ) becomes a pronouncement that the end (Heb. qēṣ) is near. The conversation in these two vision reports involves YHWH interpreting the meaning of the vision. The third vision emphasizes the certainty of YHWH's decision, and the fourth vision emphasizes the chronology of judgment: the end is near.

The fifth vision (9:1–4) breaks the pattern again. This time, the vision report contains no conversation. The prophet is merely a spectator who watches as the temple of Israel is destroyed and the inhabitants cannot escape death. Poetically and graphically the final vision describes the destruction of Israel, the northern kingdom, and its population as a fait accompli at the hands of YHWH.

These five visions represent a composition in which the pattern and the sequence of the individual vision report play a definitive role in the escalation of danger to Israel. In the current form, however, this composition has been expanded after the third and fourth vision by the insertion of a prophetic narrative (7:10–17) and a theological summary (8:4–14). The prophetic narrative serves a literary function and fits nicely into its context with its reference to the death of Jeroboam (7:11; cf. 7:9b) and the destruction of Israel/Isaac (7:16; cf. Isaac/Israel in 7:9a). The narrative's location also underscores the culpability of the religious officials of Bethel and the king of Israel. The narrative appears in precisely the place in the structure of the first two vision reports where the prophet interceded on behalf of the people, immediately after learning of the destructive purpose of the vision (see 7:2, 5).

In this third vision, not only does no intercession occur, but the narrative tells how the chief priest at Bethel conspired with Jeroboam II, the king of

Israel, to remove Amos from the land. The contrast between the intercessory activity of Amos in the first two visions and the intervention of the chief priest to the king to remove YHWH's spokesperson from the land could hardly be more powerful. Amos had twice delayed YHWH from taking action (7:3, 6), but here in the third vision Amaziah's action replaces the intercession of Amos and leads directly into the fourth vision and the announcement that the end is near.

Following the fourth vision (8:1–3), Amos 8:4–14 represents a kind of theological reflection upon the book of Amos before the final vision describes Israel's destruction. The phrases and themes of Amos 8:4–14 evoke sayings directed against Israel elsewhere in the book of Amos. The combination of unusual terms picks up phrases from both the oracle against Israel that climaxes the oracles against the nations (2:6–16) and quite a number of sayings from chapters 3–6. These recurring phrases appear in almost every verse of 8:4–14, as is evident in chart 24.[2]

Chart 24: Recurring Phrases in Amos 8 and Elsewhere in Amos

8:3: dead bodies; Hush!	6:9–10: dead bodies; Hush!
8:4: Hear this!	3:1; 4:1; 5:1: Hear this!
8:4: Trample (*šā'ap*) on the needy (*'ebyôn*)	2:7: Trampling (*šā'ap*) on the head of the poor
8:5: (abuse of sacred days)	(see the theme of 5:21–24)
8:6: buying the needy (*'ebyôn*) for a pair of sandals and taking grain (*bar*) from the needy for profit	2:6: Selling the needy (*'ebyôn*) for sandals
	5:11: taxing the poor for grain (*bar*)
8:7: Swearing by the pride of Jacob	6:8: YHWH swearing, hating the pride of Jacob
8:8: land trembles and inhabitants mourn	9:5: the earth melts and its inhabitants mourn
8:9: on that day I will make a day of light into darkness	5:18–20: The day of YHWH will become a day of darkness and not light
8:10: I will turn your feasts into mourning	5:21: I despise your festivals
Your songs become laments	5:16: farmers mourn and funeral singers will lament
8:11: famine on the land; (not a) thirst for water,	4:6: lack of bread in the cities
8:12: but wandering (*nûa'*) the land to seek (*bāqaš*) the word of YHWH	4:8: wandering (*nûa'*) for water
8:13: young maidens (*bətûlāh*) and men will faint from thirst	5:4–6: Seek (*dāraš*) YHWH and live
8:14: (from Dan to Beersheba) will fall and not rise	5:2: Maiden (*bətûlāh*) Israel has fallen, no more to rise

The language of 8:4–14 thus evokes the language and imagery of the two preceding sections, in the process creating a type of summary of the message of Amos. This message serves the function of embedding the vision reports more fully into the larger collection. Most likely, an author/editor created this summary when incorporating the vision cycle into the larger collection. Literarily, this summary causes the reader to pause between the fourth and the final vision to experience once again the accusatory power of the prophet's message of impending judgment against YHWH's own people for their utter lack of social justice (8:4–6) and their improper worship practices (8:9–10).

At the conclusion of this summary, one finds the fifth and final vision (9:1–4) and a doxology (9:5–6). The pattern of the vision report changes once again. The first two vision reports contained dialogue and intercession. While the third and fourth vision reports contained no prophetic intercession, they did contain dialogue between the prophet and YHWH. By contrast, the fifth vision contains no dialogue. It presents the prophet as a spectator who watches as YHWH destroys the thresholds and capitals of the temple of the northern kingdom. The destruction of the temple symbolizes the destruction of the entire kingdom, as is evident from the remaining verses proclaiming the impossibility of escape. The doxology punctuates the final vision report with a hymnic description of YHWH's cosmic power over creation.

Following the vision reports, the book of Amos concludes with two complex units (9:7–10, 11–15) that explore the question of Israel's survival after its destruction, something that the book has not done prior to this point. The complexity of these units concerns the internal diversity of the message, a diversity that gives rise to multiple suggestions for the genesis of these verses. In 9:7–10 one finds a discussion in two parts: the relativizing of Israel's election among the nations that culminates in a pronouncement of complete destruction (9:7–8a) and a negation of the pronouncement of complete destruction followed by the proclamation that a remnant will survive (9:8b-10).

The first part of this discussion contains a statement that rejects the proposition that Israel's election means that its fate differs substantively from any other nation. YHWH claims that his act of bringing Israel out of Egypt is no different than the salvific action he displayed toward the Philistines and the Syrians. The two parts of Amos 9:8 juxtapose contrasting pronouncements that serve as the hinge to this first complex unit. Consequently, when YHWH sees the sinful action of Israel, YHWH's past salvific deeds for Israel will not protect it from YHWH's judgment. It is YHWH who determines to destroy the kingdom from the face of the earth (9:8a).

The second half of the verse (9:8b) reverses course by relativizing the judgment: "except that I will not utterly destroy the house of Jacob." This second half of 9:8 introduces a pronouncement that the judgment will scatter Israel among the nations (9:9), while limiting the death sentence to the "sinners of my people" (9:10). Debate exists among scholars regarding whether this complex unit reflects two stages (a statement of judgment followed by a later hand offering a message of hope that a remnant will survive) or a single composition that deliberately contrasts the two positions for rhetorical effect. In either case, the juxtaposition of these two contrasting statements in the end forces the reader to engage the debate. This type of juxtaposition thus serves a didactic function, not unlike the use of contrasting aphorisms that call for two opposing responses, such as one finds in Proverbs 26:4 ("Do not answer a fool according to his folly") and 26:5 ("Answer a fool according to his folly").

The second complex unit (9:11–15) offers a promise that builds upon the idea of a surviving remnant, but it offers two different visions of hope. The complexity of the passage comes in two forms, the formal and the conceptual. First, the complex unit has two different introductory formulas (9:11, 13), which present themselves as two distinct sayings. The first formula contains a demonstrative pronoun that presupposes an antecedent (on *that* day); at least in the present context the antecedent must refer to the time of the remnant in 9:10. The formula that introduces 9:11–12 is also matched with a concluding formula at the end of 9:12 ("says the LORD who does this"). The second formula, which introduces 9:13–15 ("behold the days are coming"), is also paired with a concluding formula at the end of 9:15 ("says the LORD your God"). Hence, the concluding verses of Amos present two promises (9:11–12, 13–15) that both have a formal introduction and conclusion. It would therefore not be surprising to find that the substance of the two promises differs from one another. What is surprising, however, as noted in the previous chapter of this book, is that the nature of the promise displays not two different visions of the future but three distinct concepts of what the future holds.

Amos 9:11–12 promises restoration of the Davidic kingdom. This promise displays a hopeful future in political terms. The fallen booth of David probably refers to Jerusalem after 587 BCE and reflects a Judean vision for the future where the kingdom is once again united as in the time of David, with a Judean king in control of the surrounding nations as well as Israel (9:12). The second section of this complex unit (9:13–15) presents two different visions of the future in its current form. The more modest of these two conceptualizations appears in 9:14–15 as the restoration of normalcy. The cities that have been destroyed will be rebuilt (9:14a) and the people will again return to a life of planting and harvesting (9:14b–15).

By contrast, 9:13 portrays the future in much more utopian and hyperbolic images that offer a superabundance of the land's fertility. In this portrait, it is not enough that the land will produce again. The ones harvesting will still be at work while the planters start to sow the new crops, and the mountains and hills will drip wine. Commentaries will offer various explanations for these three distinct visions of the future, but it is clear that the book of Amos ends on an optimistic note that is unlike the message of the vast majority of the book. Most of the prophetic books end in promises, to the point that most scholars recognize this theological affirmation comes to be expected for prophetic collections: the words of the prophetic collections begin with judgment but usually affirm a promise that YHWH will prepare a way for restoration in the future for those who remain.

This overview of the collections of Amos demonstrates that the interpreter must be conscious not only of the immediate context but also must keep an ear open for the development of the larger contexts. The individual oracles against the nations in chapters 1–2 pronounce judgment upon the nations individually, but collectively they provide a rhetorical backdrop to pronounce judgment upon Israel in dramatic fashion. The incessant drumbeat of judgment sayings against Israel in chapters 3–6 drives home the prophet's message that YHWH expects social justice and expects one's actions toward one's neighbor to match one's rhetoric toward God. The vision reports in chapters 7–9 build upon one another in climactic fashion, but they pause before the final vision of destruction to rehearse the themes of the book. The concluding sections in 9:7–15 offer a series of hopeful endings that run the gamut from utter devastation to the survival of a remnant, to the restoration of the kingdom, to the rebuilding of normal life, to a utopian hope for incomprehensible agricultural fertility. The totality of these promises offers hope to YHWH's devastated people that the greatest blessings are yet to come.

6

Common Themes in Prophetic Texts

The previous chapter focused upon the relationship of literary units *to* their immediate and broader contexts. This chapter will focus on the thematic elements that run *through* a prophetic book. The previous chapter highlighted specific elements that point to different literary functions played by various prophetic textual units. This chapter will focus on thematic distinctions within prophetic books. At their core, the units that comprise prophetic books break down thematically into two types of messages: (1) negative expressions of judgment, confrontation, and warning; (2) positive words of hope, promise, and restoration. This chapter, therefore, will explore the nature of these judgment pronouncements and declarations of hope.

JUDGMENT PRONOUNCEMENTS

Judgment pronouncements occur in response to human behavior. The means of judgment typically involves some type of corporate punishment, but later prophetic texts begin to distinguish between the guilty and the innocent. Thematic categories concerning positive messages in prophetic writings generally involve the reversal of these same judgment themes. The expression of these messages in many respects mirrors one another thematically (and sometimes linguistically). To understand these judgment themes, one should recognize the causes for these pronouncements, the complicated nature of the relationship of YHWH's people with the nations, and the means of punishment described in these texts.

Causes of Judgment

In most cases, judgment pronouncements provide a rationale for YHWH's judgment. Pronouncements of judgment can be categorized thematically by their causes: ignoring social justice, improper ethical behavior, the breaking of covenants, and cultic violations.

Social Ethics: The Wealthy Oppressing the Poor

Social justice represents a major focal point of the accusations in prophetic literature, though some prophetic books emphasize these issues more than others. Expectations of justice and loyal commitment (ḥesed) as the guiding principles for society lead to pronouncements of judgment when human behavior does not match those expectations. These expectations emphasize the need for the wealthy of society to pay attention to those less fortunate and to create ethical systems that do not benefit the wealthy at the expense of the poor.

Amos 2:6–7 begins the final section of the oracles against the nations with the same refrain that appears seven times previously in 1:3–2:5 ("for three transgressions and for four I will not turn it back"), with the exception that this final climactic oracle is directed against Israel rather than a foreign nation or Judah. Rhetorically, this unit dramatically focuses the judgment upon the northern kingdom. Just as powerfully, the unit begins with a programmatic accusation of wrongdoing that sets the tone for the message of judgment that will continue nearly to the end of the book. Not until one gets to 9:7–10, 11–15 does one find any words of hope in the remainder of Amos. Rather, the opening accusation in 2:6–7 accuses the wealthy of Israel of human trafficking (selling the righteous/needy), acting with violence and impunity toward the poor (trampling on the head of the poor/pushing the destitute out of the way), and sexual impropriety (father and son enter the same woman). Similar accusations appear elsewhere in the book (5:10–11, 14–15; 6:4–7; 8:4–6), so that both the location of the charges as the first accusation against Israel and the repetition of the charges emphasize their importance. Those more fortunate because of their societal positions have an obligation to those less fortunate in society.

Micah 2:1–11 similarly condemns the wealthy of Judah at the end of the eighth century BCE for using their power and influence to take land and to expel the most vulnerable living on that land. Micah 6:8 expresses these expectations programmatically and powerfully: "He has told you, O mortal, what is good; and what does the LORD require of you but to do justice, to love kindness (ḥesed), and to walk humbly with your God?" This admonition inculcates prophetic ethical and theological expectations for those who follow YHWH.

Unethical Behavior of Individuals

Lack of civility and improper business dealings hurt the broader society. YHWH's expectations carry ethical obligations. To know God is to live lives devoid of actions that harm others, such as swearing, lying, murder, stealing, adultery, and violence (Hos. 4:1–3). These expectations also appear prominently in the Ten Commandments, but their presence (explicit and implicit) within prophetic units underscores the centrality of ethical behavior for individuals.

Numerous prophetic speeches presuppose the need for a just society that operates on rules of fairness for all. The wealthy should not gain unfair advantage because they have the wealth to bribe their way through life; the powerful should not exert their power for their own gain; the clever should not manipulate others to better their own lot (Jer. 9:23–24). Rather, to know YHWH means to live lives that are characterized by the things that please YHWH. God expects justice (*mišpāṭ*), righteousness (*ṣədāqāh*), and steadfast love (*ḥesed*). These qualities define the lives of those who know YHWH.

Similarly, prophetic claims of unethical behavior in business practices also elicit pronouncements of judgment in ways that go beyond individual acts. Society does not function well when traders are allowed to rig the system (see Hos. 12:6–7; Amos 5:12–15; 8:5) or when people are allowed to take advantage of others (Zech. 5:1–4; 7:9–12). Such behavior eats at the fabric of society, creating the need for punishment and cleansing in these prophetic paradigms.

Breaking Covenants

Another recurring theme for judgment relates to the consequences of breaking covenant. Breaking societal agreements, or covenants, appears as a major accusation in prophetic oracles in cultic, political, and theological contexts. In texts that accuse Israel or its leaders of breaking covenant, one should assess the specifics of the accusation, because breaking the covenant means different things in different texts. These differences can relate to questions regarding interpretations of individual statutes, to the breaking of political treaties, or to the broad abrogation of the Sinai covenant that is assumed to have both theological and ethical stipulations.

In some cases, the charge of breaking covenant appears to revolve around the perceived improper interpretation of specific statutes in the legal codes. For example, covenant breaking refers to improprieties of one priestly group as charged by another in the Persian-period prophetic collection of Malachi. Malachi 2:4–9 confronts a group of priests for breaking the "covenant of Levi" and teaching others to do the same (see 2:7). The implication seems clear. Disputes concerning interpretations of cultic practices lead the prophetic speaker in Malachi to confront those priests with whom he disagrees, not only for the practices themselves but for the fact that they also taught others to do so.

In another instance, Jeremiah 34:8–20, punishment comes to the king and the priests after they have gone back on their promise to free Hebrew slaves after seven years. In this instance, the breaking of the covenant that provides the rationale for judgment relates specifically to one legal statute (see Deut. 15:1).

In other texts the charge of covenant breaking refers to political treaties. Ezekiel 17 recounts a parable of two eagles. The explication of that parable (17:11–21) interprets the action using covenant language that refers to the breaking of a treaty between human kings. The passage speaks of the covenant between the king of Babylon and the king of Judah (Zedekiah) who was placed on the throne by Babylon after the previous Judean king (Jehoiachin) was taken to Babylon in the first deportation (597 BCE). Ezekiel condemns such behavior because of the impotence of the pharaoh to whom Zedekiah turns and because of the consequences it will bring in the form of retaliation from Babylon.

In Jeremiah, "covenant" can refer to the agreement made between YHWH and the people at Sinai, and several texts emphasize the first commandment to have no other gods before YHWH (Jer. 11:6–11). Relatedly, such texts may stress that the worship of other gods is condemned (11:12–13; 22:8–9). In these texts the worship of other gods by Judah and Jerusalem constitutes the grounds for Jerusalem's destruction. The fact that these texts relate in significant ways to the disregard of the first, and primary, commandment in the Decalogue should not be underestimated. In a very real sense, not only the entire Decalogue but the entire Sinai covenant rests upon the expectation that Israel shall have no other gods than YHWH. Debates exist in scholarly literature regarding how and when this emphasis upon the exclusive worship of YHWH developed in Judah and Israel, but one thing is certain. The prophetic corpus, in its final form, frequently articulates these expectations by drawing upon language of covenant, as well as other recurring thematic issues discussed below.

All of these examples, and others, indicate that the breaking of a covenant had serious consequences in prophetic literature but that the content of the covenant varied widely.

Cultic Abuses

Turning to other gods represents a charge that appears regularly in prophetic texts. It not only violates the first commandment (You shall have no other gods before me), but it also taps into theological ideas concerning the character of God as a jealous God who expects fidelity. Thus, in a number of prophetic texts prostitution serves as a metaphor for worshiping deities other than YHWH.[1] The worship of Baal plays a significant role in accusations against YHWH's people in Hosea and Jeremiah (Jer. 2:8; 7:9; 11:13, 17; 12:16; 19:5; 23:13, 27; 32:29, 35; Hos. 2:8, 16; 13:1; Zeph. 1:4). Jeremiah also condemns the worship of a goddess labeled as the Queen of Heaven (Jer. 7:18; 44:17–19, 25). These polemical texts draw a clear line in the sand for the prophets. They also indicate that there existed a more diverse religious community than most students assume when they begin studying the prophets. The numerous admonitions to keep the worship of YHWH central make little sense if competing religious systems were not represented in the country.

In a closely related theme, idolatry represents a particularly reprehensible charge among prophetic texts because it confuses the human with the divine. The absurdity of idol worship finds no more memorable treatment than in Isaiah 44:9–17. The passage begins with a fairly typical denunciation of idol worship (44:9–11), followed by descriptions of the human craftsmanship involved in making idols of metal (44:12–13) and wood (44:14). The remainder of the passage ridicules the logic of worshiping something that human hands have made. It concludes with an almost cartoonish scene describing how the carpenter cuts down a tree. He uses half of the tree to start a fire and cook his meal so that he is well fed and warm, while he uses the other half to fashion an idol to which he prays for deliverance. The vivid scene starkly demonstrates that idols have no real power.

Like texts in 1 and 2 Kings that condemn Jeroboam I of Israel (ca. 931–910 BCE) for setting up calves to worship at Bethel and Dan to keep Israelites from worshiping at Jerusalem, Hosea 8:4–6 condemns the worship of the calf in Samaria. Undoubtedly these calves were used in what the northern kingdom defined as the worship of YHWH, but later prophets did not share this perspective. In fact, the entire chapter condemns the northern kingdom for abandoning YHWH and offering sacrifice, contrary to YHWH's instruction. In Hosea 8:11–12, the prophetic voice accuses Ephraim (i.e., the northern kingdom) of multiplying altars and refusing to heed the LORD's written instruction to refrain from doing so.

Other accusations regarding improper cultic practices cover a wide range of behaviors. These actions include bringing inferior sacrificial animals, ancestor worship, and eating that which is ritually unclean. Malachi 1:6–8 challenges the priests for allowing people of Judah to bring sacrificial animals that are blind or lame, actions that run contrary to stipulations in the cultic codes (see Lev. 22:21–22). Isaiah 65:4 refers to those who spend the night in sepulchres, presumably performing rituals relating to ancestor worship, and it condemns those who are eating pork, which contradicts statutes in the Torah.

One can point to other places where attitudes toward particular Torah regulations come into play. Ezekiel accuses priests of not teaching the people how to distinguish between the clean and the unclean, thus forsaking their pedagogical task (Ezek. 22:26). Haggai 2:11–14 recounts a prophetic dialogue with a group of priests concerning cultic statutes regarding what is clean and unclean and then uses this information to draw a distinction between what has been going on and what will change (2:15–19).

Such accusations provide insights into the cultic expectations and ritual practices as they develop over time. Hence one finds a complex picture of the relationship between the prophets and the cult. At times, the prophets condemn practices taking place under the auspices of cultic officials, but none of these challenges should be interpreted as meaning that the cult and its rituals should be ignored. To the contrary, most of these challenges give clear indication that prophetic figures expected closer adherence to the full practice of YHWH's instruction, not its overthrow.

Political alliances with foreign nations are often interpreted in prophetic texts as the rejection of YHWH or YHWH's counsel. A number of prophetic texts portray the actions of particular Israelite or Judean kings as foolish and dangerous attempts to play one side against another or as the vain hope for a change in political fortunes. The hope is considered vain because it runs counter to the acts that YHWH has set in motion (Hos. 7:10–11; 9:3) and because Jerusalem has placed its trust in the power of another kingdom who cannot overpower YHWH's army (Jer. 2:36–37; Isa. 20:3–4). But rejection of foreign alliances is not the only way that the nations appear in prophetic judgment texts. Foreign nations are also the object of collections of judgment texts.

Judgment against the Nations

The relationship between Israel and the nations in the prophetic writings is complex. Nevertheless, each of the four scrolls contains material that pronounces judgment against foreign nations and material that has been collected (or composed) and grouped together. These groups of oracles against foreign nations appear as major compositional blocks in Isaiah 13–23, Jeremiah 46–51, and Ezekiel 25–32. In the Book of the Twelve, two of the twelve writings have their own collection of oracles against foreign nations (Amos 1:3–2:3; Zeph. 2:4–14). Additionally, three of the writings (Obadiah, Nahum, and Habakkuk) contain words of judgment against the foreign nations of Edom, Assyria, and Babylon respectively.

Crimes against humanity appear as accusations in a number of oracles against foreign nations. These accusations assume that YHWH will hold foreign nations accountable because boundaries of behavior exist that should not be crossed, even in times of war. Relatedly, unprovoked attacks upon unprotected populations are also condemned. For example, consider the rationales articulated in Joel 3:4–8 (MT 4:4–8) and Amos 1:3–2:3.

Joel 3:4–8 (MT 4:4–8) describes the practice of raids against Judah by Tyre, Sidon, and Philistia in which these peoples sold Judeans into slavery. In this instance, the punishment fits the crime. In Joel 3:6 (MT 4:6), the coastal regions of Philistia and Phoenicia sell Judeans as slaves to the northwest and across the ocean to the Greeks. For their punishment, YHWH will give the Phoenicians and the Philistines into the hands of Judah, who will sell them to the southeast across the desert to the Sabeans.

Amos names specific crimes in several of the oracles against foreign nations that all begin with the refrain "for three transgressions of X and for four, I will not take it back." Amos condemns Damascus for its brutality against the people of Gilead by using farm equipment as torture implements (1:3). Gaza (1:6) and Tyre (1:9) are criticized for exiling entire populations. Edom is accused of turning upon its ally, Judah (1:11). The Ammonites are accused of brutalizing pregnant women and their unborn children (1:13). Moab is accused of burning the king of Edom beyond recognition (2:1).

In other cases, however, prophetic oracles against the nations offer no clear, explicit rationale for punishment. Rather, they merely articulate unspecified, vague references to the nations taunting YHWH's people. Some collections of oracles against the nations do not mention specific charges but seem to assume that justice demands that YHWH punish these nations, just as YHWH has punished Judah and Jerusalem.

The oracles in Zephaniah 2:4–15 pronounce divine judgment against five foreign peoples (the Philistines, Moab, the Ammonites, the Cushites, and Assyria), but the only explicit rationale for the judgment appears in 2:8, where Moab and the Ammonites are accused of taunts and boasts against Judah. The oracle against Assyria indirectly, but quite vaguely, portrays Nineveh as guilty of arrogance (2:15). This charge hardly seems to warrant, by itself, the pronouncement of destruction that one finds in 2:13–15, unless one imports knowledge of Assyrian oppression from outside Zephaniah. Importing such knowledge may not be difficult for Assyria, given the anti-Assyrian polemic one finds in places like Isaiah 9–10 and Nahum 2–3. Nevertheless, finding a meaningful rationale for this judgment requires going beyond the text as we have it. Ben Zvi and Berlin have plausibly suggested that all of the nations mentioned in this collection benefited from the expansion of Assyrian power in the eighth and seventh century, but they would lose those economic benefits when Assyria departed the scene in the latter part of the seventh century.[2] Isaiah 13–23 and Jeremiah 46–51 generally contain much more description of punishment than they do accusations against the nations who are destroyed. Consider, for example, Isaiah 13–14. These two lengthy chapters pronounce judgment against Babylon, but the language only periodically alludes to the cause of their punishment, because Babylon's wicked rulers oppressed other nations (14:5–6) or because of its arrogance (14:13). In this respect, then, these collections of oracles against foreign nations have more to say as affirmations of YHWH's divine power than about specific crimes committed by nations. By reiterating the certainty that foreign nations will experience punishment at the hands of YHWH, these collections function as reminders of YHWH's universal control. YHWH has the power to use Assyria or Babylon to punish Judah (cf. Isa. 10:5–11; Hab. 1:5–11), but in the end YHWH will use that power to punish the Assyrians and the Babylonians as well (Isa. 10:12; Hab. 3:16).

Types of Judgment

While the themes mentioned above relate to the reasons for judgment, one should note that the means of punishment in prophetic literature tend to be corporate in nature. Three types of punishment predominate, though a fourth type plays a significant, albeit smaller, role. The three dominant types are YHWH's use of a foreign nation to punish Israel and Judah, YHWH's use of natural disasters as a means of punishment, and YHWH's direct intervention to inflict punishment. These forms of punishment affect the entire community indiscriminately. Only occasionally do prophetic texts pronounce judgment against specific individuals, but this fourth type of punishment, that is, punishing only those who are guilty, begins to play a significant role in later prophetic texts.

Foreign Nations as Instruments of Punishment

Prophetic texts assume that YHWH uses foreign nations and foreign kings to punish the people and leaders of Judah and Israel. Perhaps the most famous example appears in Isaiah 10:5–6, where YHWH proclaims Assyria to be the "rod" of his anger, by which he intends to punish Israel and Judah, even though YHWH knows that the king of Assyria will attempt to extend his power beyond what YHWH will allow (10:7). One can also illustrate this means of punishment in Habakkuk, where the prophetic speaker begins by proclaiming the enduring problem of injustice and violence that the people of Judah commit against one another (Hab. 1:2–4). In "response" YHWH announces plans to send the Babylonians (1:5–11). Similarly, the threat of the "enemy from the north" appears early in the book of Jeremiah and plays a dominant role throughout the remainder of the book.[3] What these and other pronouncements share is the idea that YHWH will send an insurmountable foe against YHWH's own people to punish the nation for things it has done.

Natural Calamities

In other instances, prophetic texts assume that YHWH will use natural calamities as punishment against Judah and Israel. Amos 4:6–11 describes a sequence of such calamities, including famine, drought, blight, mildew, locust plagues, and pestilence, that YHWH intended as chastisement to force Israel to change its ways. But in each case YHWH recounts the plaintive refrain: "yet you did not return to me, says YHWH." (4:6, 8, 9, 10, 11). The first chapter of Joel begins with a series of imperatives calling for the people to turn to YHWH in response to a series of devastations that includes locust plagues, drought, and military attack. These calls assume that the people have done something contrary to YHWH's will that has brought about these signs of curse from YHWH.[4]

YHWH's Direct Intervention

A number of texts describe YHWH's direct intervention to punish the nation or the foreign nations, but only two will be mentioned here as illustrations. This type of judgment generally takes the form of a theophany report or draws upon the tradition of YHWH as divine warrior. Theophany reports announce YHWH's appearance in cosmic terms. Consider Micah 1:2–7. The prophetic speaker announces YHWH will leave his heavenly abode in order to appear on earth (1:2–3a). The earth, however, will not be able to withstand his appearance. The mountains will melt like wax as YHWH tramples across the tops of them (1:4). Samaria and Jerusalem are then identified as the target of his coming judgment (1:5–7). Other examples of theophany reports include hymns like Nahum 1:2–8 (against Nineveh) and visions such as Jeremiah 23:18–20.

Several texts take the idea of a theophany even further and portray YHWH as a warrior who comes to do battle against a specific enemy or against the nations. Often these texts draw upon Judah's adaptation of traditions of chaos battle motifs from the ancient Near Eastern creation myths. In these contexts, the hostile forces (usually the nations) array themselves for battle against YHWH, but YHWH overpowers them. These texts usually include references to the Sea (Yam) and the River (Nahar), two primary characters in the version of this chaos battle found in the Baal myth. Consider Habakkuk 3:3–15, which begins with a theophany report (3:3–7) in which YHWH comes, the earth and the mountains tremble, and the nations fear (3:6). Further depictions take the form of a victory song and draw upon the chaos battle against the Sea (Yam) and the River (Nahar). These entities represent the powers of chaos at creation, who are no match for YHWH and who are defeated (3:10). Then the text also refers to a particular enemy who acted against YHWH's people (3:13–14) but who will be defeated along with the nations and the chaos powers. Debate exists whether this victory hymn was composed specifically for Habakkuk or whether it was placed here by editors to affirm YHWH's ultimate power, thereby assuming that readers would associate the enemy of the poem with Babylon. Either way, the entire hymn functions as an affirmation that YHWH would eventually overpower Babylon (the enemy), even though Judah would be punished first (3:16).

Isaiah 34 draws heavily upon images of YHWH as divine warrior. The passage depicts YHWH's anger as directed against all the nations (34:2) whom he has doomed to slaughter using the power of his sword (34:5) before he turns his attention to destroying Edom (34:5–7). The warrior's battle against Edom is motivated by vengeance for Zion (34:8). The consequences of the divine warrior's defeat of Edom are described in graphic detail (34:9–15) as complete devastation. This image of the future destruction of Edom on a "day of vengeance" (34:8) is presupposed in Isaiah 63:1–7, where YHWH is returning from Edom (63:1) with blood all over him (63:2–3, 6), after his arm has brought victory sustained by his own wrath (63:5) on "the day of vengeance" (63:4). Whereas Isaiah 34 presumes the future battle against Edom and the nations, the account in 63:1–7 describe those events as having already occurred.

The role of YHWH as divine warrior is pervasive but varied. The motif of the divine warrior plays a prominent role in prophetic eschatological texts, but the details have to be assessed in each text. The battle may be described in cosmic terms as the hostile nations of the world (Isa. 34:2) or in political terms as specific nations (Isa. 34:5). The motif can also create expectations for the return of the warrior to Jerusalem as king after the victorious battle (Zeph. 3:14–17). It can be drawn upon to describe the warrior/king exercising his kingly role as judge (Joel 3:9–17 [MT 4:9–17]). YHWH's army can include the heavenly host (Joel 3:11 [MT 4:11]) or the people of Judah and Israel (Zech. 9:13).

The target of YHWH's military campaign most often appears as foreign nations, but YHWH can also attack his own people (Joel 2:1–11). In addition to the two texts illustrated above, one could also include other eschatological passages where the divine warrior, king, and judge come into play. For example, the divine warrior/king plays a role in the assumption of the victorious warrior in Isaiah 49:22; 51:9–11; 52:7–10; 66:15–16; in battling Gog, the leader of the hostile nations who attack YHWH, the leader of the army of his people (Ezek. 38:1–23); in the protection of YHWH's land (Zech. 9:1–8}; and in the battle against the nations (Zech. 14:1–21). These texts can vary significantly in terms of who is battling YHWH, the presence/absence of an army, the weapons used by YHWH, and the depiction of the battle and its aftermath. What unites them is the idea that YHWH will intervene directly against the forces of evil.

Corporate and Individual Fate

Periodically, prophetic texts begin to show a certain level of discomfort with the idea that punishment affects the entire country, not just the people who are guilty. This fourth perspective begins to find articulation in texts from the exilic period onward, and it takes several forms. For example, Amos 9:7–10 records both sides of a debate. This text is frequently attributed to an exilic editor who seeks to offer some measure of comfort to those who have survived YHWH's judgment. The first portion of this passage (9:7–8a) rejects the notion that YHWH's election of Israel provides them any protection from judgment. The passage implies that Israel means no more to YHWH than the Ethiopians, the Philistines, or the Syrians. This portion of the text culminates in the definitive pronouncement from YHWH: "I will destroy it [the sinful kingdom] from the face of the earth" (9:8a). The second half of this discussion begins immediately thereafter by undercutting that definitive statement with one offering a word of hope that some will survive when it says, "Nevertheless, I will not utterly destroy the house of Jacob" (9:8b). Verses 9–10 go on to describe the judgment in terms of a sieve, so that while the entire house of Israel will experience punishment, only "the sinners of my people" will die.

Material in both Jeremiah and Ezekiel addresses the exilic community over a similar issue, though in slightly different ways. Ezekiel 18:2 pointedly challenges the proverb used by some to explain why children were suffering in the aftermath of Jerusalem's destruction and the exile of much of its population. The parable seems clear: "the parents have eaten sour grapes, and the children's teeth are set on edge." In other words, there were people who were saying that the younger generation must suffer for the sins of their parents. Most of the remainder of this chapter directly challenges this theology by rejecting its claim and stating categorically that "only the person who sins shall die" (18:4).

By contrast, Jeremiah 31:29–30 reflects a more ambiguous approach to the issue, in that it offers a hope for a future time when people will no longer repeat this proverb. In other words, the proverb represents a present reality that these verses do not reject outright. The text, rather, assumes that YHWH's punishment of Jerusalem was just because of the crime (the sins of the fathers), but it offers hope that the future will bring relief. These verses in Jeremiah, in fact, come immediately before the famous new covenant passage (31:31–34), which anticipates a time when all those in Israel will internalize YHWH's instruction: "I will put my instruction within them, and I will write it on their hearts" (31:33). While these two units may or may not have been composed simultaneously, their placement alongside one another offers a theological touchstone that can hardly be missed. A time is coming when everyone will be able to discern YHWH's instruction. It may require a radical reorientation, but both passages express a deep longing for a change in circumstance.

Isaiah and the Book of the Twelve also reflect pieces of this dialogue. Near the end of both scrolls, texts appear that emphasize a change in the way YHWH's judgment will be exercised. In both cases, future judgment will be exacted upon those who have committed evil, while the righteous will escape judgment. Malachi 4:1–2 (MT 3:19–20) describes the coming day of YHWH in precisely these terms when it speaks of the evildoers and the arrogant who will be punished like those burning in an oven, while those fearing YHWH shall experience the same events as "the sun of righteousness" that comes with "healing in its wings" and allows them to rise up and go forth. In other words, YHWH's judgment will distinguish between the righteous and the wicked. Similarly, Isaiah 66 anticipates not a time that divides between YHWH's nation and foreigners but a time when deliverance will come to all those who are humble, contrite in spirit, and trembling at YHWH's word (66:2). By contrast, YHWH's judgment will come against those who have chosen their own way and who delight in the abominations they perform (66:3), actions that YHWH considers evil (66:4). At this time, even the foreign nations will have survivors who shall come and worship in Jerusalem, and depending upon how one interprets the pronouns, some from among those nations may even become priests and Levites (see 66:18–21).

These texts, and others, begin to wrestle with the theological ramifications of concepts of God's judgment that are tied closely to the fate of a single nation. They struggle with images of divine wrath that do not adequately speak to the survivors of Jerusalem's destruction. They look for ways to affirm the need for fidelity to the ways of YHWH—and thus avoiding judgment—while simultaneously affirming this commitment to YHWH as a reason for moving forward. This unease with portraying YHWH merely as the protector of righteousness also helps to account for the fact that each of the four prophetic scrolls offers a message of hope, promise, and restoration. Judgment that leads solely to destruction cannot have the final word in the prophetic corpus.

DECLARATIONS OF HOPE

As already noted, while the vast majority of prophetic texts deal with issues of judgment, no prophetic writing in its final form ends without some form of hope for restoration. In fact, the themes of hope, restoration, and promise essentially function as counterthemes to the images of judgment that appear within the prophetic writings. Restoration appears in words of hope and promise that have political connotations, that restore the relationships ruptured by the people's behavior, that reverse the types of punishment, and that create literary reversals for figures upon whom judgment was pronounced.

Physical and Political Restoration

A number of prophetic texts focus upon physical and political restoration, but different contexts display different rhetorical agendas. Evaluating the clues to these contexts represents one of the basic historical tasks for those reading prophetic texts closely. For example, consider both the similarities and the differences among the following texts that promise restoration: Amos 9:11–12, 14; Isaiah 44:24–28; Haggai 2:20–23; and Obadiah 19–20.

Amos 9:11–12, 14 likely represents the core of an exilic addition to the book of Amos. This passage refers to the "fallen booth of David" (9:11) and the "ruined cities" (9:14) that YHWH will rebuild. A significant majority of critical scholars see in these terms a clear allusion to the destruction of Jerusalem and Judah in 587. These verses offer a clear promise of physical rebuilding, as well as retribution against Edom and other nations who participated in Judah's destruction (9:12). Verse 11 assumes the Davidic kingdom and its capital city of Jerusalem have fallen, but YHWH promises to restore Jerusalem to its former glory, while 9:14 expands the promise to restore "all the fortunes of my people Israel," which includes rebuilding and reinhabiting the cities that have been destroyed. Interestingly, while it promises of restoration of the "booth of David" (i.e., Jerusalem), it does not specifically associate this restoration with restoring a Davidic monarch to the throne. One may, perhaps, infer the restoration of a Davidic monarch, but the text itself leaves that promise ambiguous.

Isaiah 44:24–28 offers another promise of restoration, but with a very different perspective of how that change will occur. The passage is widely recognized as part of the core texts in Isaiah 40–55, set initially in Babylon during the exilic period. In the larger context, restoration is portrayed as a return to Jerusalem across the wilderness (e.g., 40:3). Within 44:24–28, restoration is perceived as the rebuilding of Jerusalem and Judah (44:26), as well as the rebuilding of the temple (44:28), a promise that is not explicit in Amos 9:11–12, 14. Amazingly, however, not only is Isaiah 44:24–28 reticent about the role of the Davidic monarchy; it depicts Cyrus, king of Persia (539–530 BCE), as the "shepherd" whom YHWH has chosen. This term frequently has royal connotations, and there can be little doubt that this text recognizes the Persian emperor as the monarch who will begin the process of restoration. This concrete reference to a specific, foreign king acting on YHWH's behalf for the people of Judah recognizes implicitly the changed realities of the international situation.

A third illustration of a prophetic promise that carries political expectations appears in Haggai 2:20–23. The setting of this text in Haggai comes after a passage that presumes that the reconstruction of the temple has already begun (2:18–19) and that people are once again living in Jerusalem (1:4). Hence, the rhetoric in Haggai focuses neither upon returning nor upon rebuilding the city, but upon rebuilding the temple. Once that process has begun, however, the book's concluding unit (2:20–23) promises two things, both of which reflect potentially volatile political perspectives. The first of these promises predicts nothing short of the upheaval of the existing world order, when YHWH will "overthrow the throne of the kingdoms" (2:21). The second promise stands out just as dramatically, once one understands its claim that Zerubbabel is the "servant" whom YHWH has "chosen."

The political connotations of this promise can hardly be missed when one recognizes two additional pieces of information. First, Zerubbabel is the grandson of Jehoiachin, the Davidic king who was exiled to Babylon in 597 BCE. Second, the claim in Haggai 2:23 that YHWH will make Zerubbabel "like a signet ring" represents a strong political statement regarding David's scion. The promise reverses an oracle of Jeremiah that YHWH was removing royal authority from Jehoiachin and the Davidic line (Jer. 22:24–27). In the perspective of Haggai, restoration cannot be complete without a monarch representing the Davidic line in Judah and Jerusalem. Quite likely, such sentiments did not sit well with Darius II, the king of Persia, who had only recently come to power. Zerubbabel never became king; neither did any other descendant of David wrest power from the Persians or the Greeks that followed them. Still other texts manifest the expectation that a descendant of David will continue to play a role in ruling the kingdom (e.g., Isa. 4:2; Jer. 33:14–18; Ezek. 34:24; 37:24–25). The number of prophetic texts articulating this line of thought remains rather low, but it does appear (see the treatment of messianic promises in chap. 4).

Finally, Obadiah 19–20 offers yet another portrait of restoration with political overtones. This passage has been interpreted as both an exilic text and a late postexilic addition to the core text of Obadiah. There is no doubt that the book of Obadiah itself reflects upon the events of Jerusalem's destruction and condemns Edom for taking part in those events as an ally of Babylon (see especially the reference to entering the gate on the day of Judah's disaster in Obad. 13 and Edom's treacherous ally in v. 7). In either case, the context of the unit (vv. 15a, 16–21) portrays the restoration of Judah and Jerusalem in retributive and territorial terms. Unlike Obadiah 1–14, 15b, which focuses its message directly upon the fate of Edom, the remainder of Obadiah promises punishment for all the nations who took advantage of Judah and Jerusalem in the aftermath of its destruction.

The day of YHWH is announced (v. 15), but this time the judgment of this day will be directed "against all the nations," including Edom. Those on Mount Zion will, however, escape (v. 16). Verses 19–20 describe a sequence of territorial repossessions that, conceptually, describes the retaking of territory that encircles Jerusalem. As though Jerusalem lay at the center of the kingdom, surrounding Judean populations expand outward, capturing territory in the south (the Negev possesses Edom), the southwest and north (the Shephelah possesses the Philistines and Ephraim/Samaria), and the northeast (Benjamin will possess Gilead). Verse 20 essentially describes a second wave in which exiles from Jerusalem and Israel living elsewhere retake territory to the Phoenician border in the north and fill in the Negev (whose population would push out Edom) in the south. This poetic depiction of territorial expansion effectively recreates the borders of the Davidic kingdom. Yet nothing in this text describes a monarch or a Davidic representative of any kind. The action in Obadiah 19–20 portrays the consequence of the day of YHWH in a more theocratic conceptualization of the kingdom: this repossession results from the action of YHWH, not a royal figure.

One can determine several things regarding restoration texts from the exilic period onward. First, the prevalence of texts offering hope for restoration within prophetic collections infers a conviction that is theologically profound, namely, that despite the fulfillment of judgment against Judah and Jerusalem in 587 BCE, YHWH has neither completely annihilated his people nor abandoned them to their own devices. All prophetic scrolls contain words of hope that are addressed to a people whose kingdom had been devastated. In fact, passages of restoration appear in every prophetic writing, whether the prophet for whom the writing is named worked during the monarchic era or later. Stated differently, those who transmitted these prophetic collections could not allow them to give the impression that YHWH had abandoned his people forever, even if some prophetic writings (e.g., Amos and Zephaniah) probably contained only messages of judgment in their earliest forms.

Second, one can detect stages of hope for a restored kingdom as well as different expectations regarding what restoration looked like. One cannot assume that these stages represent a continuous line of increasing optimism. One need only read some of the problems described in Isaiah 56–66 (containing many of the latest portions of the book) to realize that the message of hope in these chapters was also tempered by renewed calls for change. Still, one can assume that words of hope that the cities would be rebuilt and reinhabited generally predate passages that assume a functioning temple.

Third, most of these passages of hope for a restored kingdom have difficulty reincorporating a Davidic king. This relative lack of prominence of a Davidic king, even in texts that anticipate the restoration of the ideal borders of the Davidic kingdom, in all likelihood reflects both certain prophetic traditions that remain skeptical of monarchial power and the changing social, military, and political forces that developed during the Persian period. The decreased prominence of Davidic kings reflects the fact that the Persian Empire controlled the region, meaning they appointed governors and other functionaries who were responsible to the Persian monarch. Apart from Zerubbabel, mentioned in Haggai above, the Persians did not appear to have any particular affinity toward the appointment of Davidic descendants. Simultaneously, and probably to serve its own interests, Persia does support a temple system that continues to grow in power, prestige, and wealth over the two centuries of Persian hegemony. Traditions and images associated with the Davidic monarchy are often reappropriated in ways that emphasize the kingship of YHWH rather than humans. These theocratic impulses (which also appear in the Psalter) play a prominent role in the promises in the prophetic corpus. The kingdom belongs to YHWH, and YHWH will return to Jerusalem. From there, YHWH will defeat the enemies and/or lead armies into battle.

Restoring What Was Broken

Restoration texts offer hope that behavior can change. In demonstrable ways, several texts offer hope that those actions that had caused YHWH's judgment could be overcome. These texts speak not so much of new buildings but of new starts. To illustrate, consider texts that reverse the consequences of the accusations against YHWH's people. While YHWH's people broke the covenant repeatedly, YHWH offers to restore a new covenant, one that could be internalized. While cultic abuses brought judgment that destroyed the temple and the cult, renewing the cult involves a new temple and a new cultic structure.

New Covenant (Jeremiah 31)

While not pervasive in the sense of the quantity of texts in which it appears, the way in which prophetic promises reverse the themes of prophetic judgment should also take note of the famous new covenant passage in Jeremiah 31:31–34. The larger context places this passage in the context of the so-called Book of Consolation comprising chapters 30–33. This passage represents the single largest portion of Jeremiah offering words of hope to Judah and Jerusalem following Jerusalem's destruction.

Of course, the new covenant cannot be completely understood without assessing the nature of the former covenant with which it contrasts. In this respect, Jeremiah 31:32 explicitly describes this former covenant as the Sinai covenant when it says, "It will not be like the covenant that I made with their ancestors when I took them by the hand to bring them out of the land of Egypt—a covenant which they broke, though I was their husband." Yet scholars have noted how reference to the Sinai covenant has been punctuated with oblique allusions to the worship of Baal as well. The final phrase of Jeremiah 31:32 actually uses a verbal form of *bāʿal* in the phrase that the NRSV translates "though I was their husband" (*waʾānōkî bāʿaltî bām*). These undertones thereby subtly link the breaking of the Sinai covenant with the worship of other deities, a theme that is particularly dominant in Jeremiah and Hosea.

The new covenant, by contrast, will be a way of life in which fidelity to YHWH becomes an internalized reality: "I will put my law within them, and I will write it on their hearts" (31:33). Consequently, because they have internalized this knowledge, the task of teaching people to understand the ways of YHWH will no longer be necessary, because they will all know YHWH and YHWH will not hold their sin against them (31:34).

Renewal of the Cult

Several restoration texts deal with issues related to rebuilding the Jerusalem temple, as well as the restoration of cultic practices, through purification and the advocating of specific structural components within the temple bureaucracy. The decision to rebuild the temple in Jerusalem was not without controversy, yet several texts use this goal as a rallying cry for changing the relationship of the people to YHWH. Emphasis on rebuilding the temple appears in Ezekiel 40–48 and Haggai. Programmatic and polemical agendas can be seen in texts such as Zechariah 1:8–17; 3:1–10; 4:1–14; Malachi 1:6–2:9; Isaiah 56:1–8; 65:1–7.

Rebuilding the temple and its structures represents both a fulfillment of promises and the locus of ongoing debates. Ezekiel 40–48 places a major emphasis upon rebuilding the temple. This vision report, set in the twenty-fifth year after the first exile in 597 BCE, according to 40:1, begins with an extensive visionary description of the dimensions of the temple complex, its buildings, and its altars. One quickly realizes, however, that the nature of this vision report is theological, not practical. The dimensions it provides do not constitute blueprints and could hardly provide adequate guidance to carpenters and other artisans, since the temple description contains only two-dimensional measurements, not three.

The purpose of the prophet's description was never intended for these workers. It presents itself as the vision of a prophet and priest who wants to communicate that the time for a fresh start has begun. The climax of this opening section (chaps. 40–44) comes in Ezekiel 43, when the "glory of YHWH" returns to the temple from the east (43:1–3). This vision of the return reverses the vision recounted thirty-two chapters earlier when, as part of Jerusalem's judgment, the prophet described the "glory of YHWH" leaving the temple and heading to the east (11:22–23). Despite this prophetic vision that dates itself to 572 BCE, it would take fifty more years before serious work on reconstructing the temple began, and the temple that was built bore little resemblance to the one described in Ezekiel. Ezekiel 40–48 should not be understood as a prediction that was literally fulfilled but as a composition designed to provide hope for a Jewish community exiled in Babylon. It provided an ideal toward which to strive, one that probably helped to maintain the prophetic community's identity as YHWH worshipers living in a foreign land.

When the actual physical work of rebuilding the temple did finally begin, the impetus appears to have come about through the leadership of two prophetic figures, Haggai and Zechariah. The book of Haggai is not presented as a vision account like Ezekiel but as a series of vignettes arranged chronologically that testifies to the role that the message of Haggai played in exhorting the governor and the high priest to marshal the resources necessary to begin the construction of the temple in 520 BCE. Again, the decision to rebuild the temple was not a foregone conclusion, according to the book of Haggai. While some texts indicate that the initial wave of returnees had attempted to build a temple in Jerusalem in the aftermath of Cyrus of Persia's rise to power after 538 BCE and his subsequent decision to allow exiles from Babylon to return to Jerusalem (see Ezra 1–2), these efforts seem to have failed to accomplish their goal until the work of Haggai began in the fall of 520 BCE.[5]

At that point, however, Haggai's first recorded speech chides the people for not rebuilding the temple: "These people say the time has not yet come to rebuild the LORD's house. . . . Is it a time for you yourselves to live in your paneled houses, while this house lies in ruins?" (1:2, 4). As the prophet's speech continues, he implies that the people still live under judgment because they have not rebuilt YHWH's temple (1:6, 8–11). The sign of judgment, according to this speech, can be seen in YHWH's sending a drought until the temple is restored (1:9–10). Zerubbabel, who is the governor and the grandson of the last Davidic king, and the high priest Joshua respond positively to Haggai's speech and organize the people to begin working on the project (1:12–15). Once the cornerstone is laid, Haggai marks the day as the point at which Judah's fortune will change (2:18–19). The sign of that change will take the form of a restoration of the land's fertility. Note that the restoration once again takes the form of reversing the means of judgment (the prophet claimed the drought marked the sign of judgment, so the sign of restoration is not the completed temple but the removal of the drought).

Other prophetic texts show concern for cultic issues. A number of texts in Zechariah also deal with the issue of rebuilding the temple or with the way in which the temple will function. Some of these texts may be classified as programmatic, while others may be polemical. Programmatic texts tend to present their message as part of larger restoration models. Such texts would include several of Zechariah's eight vision reports. The first of these visions (1:8–17) reveals a report from YHWH's messengers that the world is at rest (1:11); so YHWH announces his decision to return to Jerusalem (1:14), to punish the nations for taking advantage of Judah (1:15), and to rebuild the temple (1:16).

Similar ideas are expressed in other prophetic books with nonvisionary genres (e.g., Jer. 33:10–11). Zechariah's fourth vision (3:1–10) concerns the cleansing and reconsecration of the chief priest Joshua, while the fifth vision (4:1–14) portrays a twofold power structure for the temple, involving both Joshua, representing the priesthood, and Zerubbabel (who is also a descendant of David), representing the civil authority. Despite this vision for the role of Zerubbabel, the bulk of the evidence across the Old Testament suggests that the priesthood retained control of the temple structures during the Persian period, while the role of David's descendants decreased rapidly.

A number of prophetic texts take up the question of how the second temple will function in more polemical terms. Most of these texts presume a functioning temple, but they reflect debates concerning cultic practices currently being employed, both inside and outside the temple. Consider three examples: the disputations of Malachi, Isaiah 56:1–8, and Isaiah 65:1–7.

Malachi contains a series of six disputations, the second and longest of which (1:6–2:9) confronts both the priests and the people for the laxity of their approach to presenting sacrifices to YHWH. Certain people bring defective animals, thus violating decrees in the Torah, but the prophet directs the harshest invective against the priests who accept such sacrifices (1:6–8). The prophet even states it would be better to shut down the temple completely, rather than to allow this practice to continue. The prophet accuses these priests of breaking the "covenant of Levi" (2:4, 8). On one level, this disputation hardly seems like a restoration text, but if—as many have argued—the date of the core of Malachi can be considered the middle of the fifth century, then this passage demonstrates that barely a generation after the rebuilding of the second temple (completed in 515 BCE), prophets were again challenging the way that priests administered their duties. A number of scholars consider Malachi to be both a priest and a prophet, not unlike Ezekiel before him (Ezek. 1:3).

In all likelihood, these debates reflect ongoing tensions in the early restoration period regarding how the cultic personnel would be structured and governed. In this sense they reflect ongoing debates that should be factored into one's understanding of the realities on the ground that go beyond the more programmatic texts.

Isaiah 56:1–8 represents a text that manifests both programmatic and polemical elements. The programmatic aspect derives from the content of the speech that attempts to create space for foreigners and eunuchs among those keeping Sabbath in the temple. The polemical tone of this inclusive text stems from the fact that it directly controverts a passage in the Torah, Deuteronomy 23:1–3, that explicitly excludes from the temple assembly those with mutilated sexual organs, Ammonites, and Moabites. Debates about whether and how foreigners could participate in worship in the Second Temple period surface directly and indirectly from the fifth century onward. Ezra and Nehemiah take a hard line against foreigners in the fifth century; yet texts such as Isaiah 56:1–8; Malachi 1:10–14; and the books of Jonah and Ruth problematize the issue from the other side.

At other times, polemical texts in the restoration period confront religious practices being performed by at least some persons outside the temple. For example, Isaiah 65:1–7 condemns those who offer sacrifice outside the temple (65:3), who spend the night in tombs among the dead, probably reflecting some type of worship practice that also involves the consumption of pork and other ritually unclean elements (65:4). Such texts suggest that the prophetic critique of priestly behavior was more concerned with the proper performance of temple worship than it was with a fundamental critique of the system. The roles of prophet and priest were not polar opposites.

The Types of Punishment Reversed

Judgment texts in prophetic literature portray judgment through various means (e.g., the sending of natural calamities, and YHWH's sending/allowing a foreign nation to conquer Judah), and portrayals of restoration often assume that restoration means reversing the consequences of these acts of judgment. Such is particularly the case with the renewal of the land's fertility and the punishment of the nations that have tormented Judah. Additionally, other themes can play upon literary contexts to anticipate restoration in terms of the reversal of judgment imagery, as in the presentation of Hosea's children (Hos. 1–2) and the restoration of Zion personified (in a number of texts). While such reversals are important aspects of restoration within prophetic texts, they can be mentioned here only very briefly as illustrations.

Fertility of the Land Restored

A number of texts, particularly in the Book of the Twelve, depict restoration as a reversal of the curse of the land's infertility. Amos 9:13–15 presents two distinct scenarios. The first, and probably earlier of the two, anticipates a time of agricultural normalcy. In 9:14b, hope is simply described as the ability to plant and to harvest. Combined with the hope of rebuilding the ruined cities of Judah in 9:14a, this expectation of a normal crop cycle leads to YHWH's affirmation that ends the book: "I will plant them upon their land, and they shall never again be plucked up out of the land that I have given them" (9:15).

By contrast, the promise of 9:13 articulates a much more utopian vision of the fertility of the land, in which the abundance of the harvest is so great that the people will still be harvesting when it is time to plow the land again, and they will still be crushing the grapes when it is time to plant seed. The fact that 9:13b contains a parallel to the later text in Joel 3:18 (MT 4:18) strongly suggests that this utopian image enters Amos at the point when the Twelve were coming together as an arranged, edited collection in their own right.

A series of texts in Haggai, Zechariah, and Malachi anticipates a time of restoration in terms of agricultural bounty. Haggai 2:15–19 calls upon the people to evaluate the change that will happen once the temple foundation has been laid. The image concerns the amount of harvest taken in previously, when the people were suffering the effects of blight, mildew, and hail because YHWH's house remained in ruins. This text appears to allude to Amos 4:6–11. The point of the passage comes in Haggai 2:19, when YHWH announces he will bless the people by changing the situation.

Another text, in Zechariah, appears as part of a collection dated two years after Haggai 2:15–19 (cf. Zech. 7:1 and Hag. 2:10). Zechariah 8:9–12 alludes back to Haggai 2:15–19 and claims that things have already improved but will get better still. Note that 8:10 refers to "before those days," 8:11 relates to "now," and 8:12 begins "and it will be." This chronological framework thus refers to the past, present, and future to anticipate a continuation of the renewal of the land's production *because* temple construction has begun.

Finally, in Malachi 3:10–12, after a disputation against the people for not providing the tithe, Malachi 3:10 challenges them to do so in order to test YHWH's ability to fulfill his promises (3:10a), send rain as an agricultural blessing (3:10b), and remove "the devourer" (3:11, NRSV "the locust"). The polemical tenor of the passage suggests that the prophetic speaker does not believe that the people have remained faithful in their obligations. To the degree that one treats these texts as interrelated in the reading of the Book of the Twelve, the reader is left with the impression that (once again) Judah has turned its back on YHWH. While the people repented following the initial work of Haggai and Zechariah (see especially Zech. 1:2–6; cf. the date in Zech. 1:1 with dates of Hag. 2:1, 10), their commitment has changed dramatically in the presuppositions of Malachi. Consequently, this motif plays out across these three writings as a type of story thread when one isolates the passages containing this imagery. The change of attitude by the people manifested in Haggai and Zechariah gives way to the polemical challenge of Malachi for failing to remain faithful to their commitment.

Punishment of the Nations

YHWH's use of foreign nations represented a second means by which YHWH punished Judah, according to many of the judgment oracles in the prophetic writings discussed earlier in this chapter. The reversal of this means of punishment probably plays some role in the fact that all four prophetic scrolls (Isaiah, Jeremiah, Ezekiel, and Book of the Twelve) contain collections of oracles directed not against Judah or Israel but against individual nations. Most of these collections either arose after Jerusalem's destruction or were updated in the aftermath of that event. Isaiah 13–23, Jeremiah 46–51, and Ezekiel 25–32 constitute major compilations of oracles directed against individual peoples surrounding Judah and Israel. The Book of the Twelve contains three writings that largely condemn one particular nation: Nahum takes aim at Assyria; Habakkuk announces both the arrival and the downfall of Babylon; and Obadiah condemns Edom for its role as an ally to Babylon and anticipates its downfall as the first of many nations to be punished on the day of YHWH. In addition, three other writings in the Book of the Twelve contain significant sections that can be classified as oracles against the nations (Amos 1:3–2:3; Zeph. 2:4–15; Zech. 9:1–8; 14:9–19). The rhetorical purpose that binds together these collections hinges upon justice from the perspective of Judah. The logic proceeds from the premise that every nation will experience punishment if they disobey YHWH's expectations.

This expectation of justice is often implicit in these oracles against foreign nations, but occasionally texts make this expectation explicit, as in Jeremiah 25:12–29 and Obadiah 15a and 16–21. These texts indicate both that YHWH must punish Jerusalem and that the time of punishment will then be transferred to other nations, when they will be forced to drink from YHWH's cup of wrath. Both of these texts proclaim recompense to the nations: just as you have done to YHWH's people, YHWH will do to you (Jer. 25:14; Obad. 15b, 16).

Returning of the People to YHWH

Judah's exile from Jerusalem (or Israel's exile from its land) and YHWH's departure from the city represent further themes that are also reversed in restoration texts. Texts announcing exile as punishment for YHWH's people or addressed to people in exile can be found in each of the four prophetic scrolls: for example, Isaiah 5:13; 27:8; Jeremiah 24:1; 29:7; Ezekiel 1:1–2; Amos 5:27, 6:7; Micah 1:16. Counterparts to this idea naturally occur in restoration texts by anticipating the return of those in exile or scattered among the nations. Some of these texts appear to presume pronouncements of return from exile in Babylon (e.g., Isa. 40:1–11; 44:24–26; Jer. 24:5–7; 30:8–11; Ezek. 36:33–36; Amos 9:11–15; Zeph. 3:19–20), while other texts speak of a wider diaspora (Isa. 43:5–7; Jer. 32:36–41; Joel 3:4–8 [MT 4:4–8]; Zech. 10:6–12).

Literary Reversals

Several restoration texts offer promises using literary figures that were involved in prophetic rhetoric of judgment. The concept of Jerusalem portrayed as Lady Zion and the symbolic names of the children of Hosea offer two good examples of these literary reversals in prophetic texts.

Lady Zion

The personified city plays a significant role in prophetic texts as wife and mother. The figure of the personified city has a long history in West Semitic cultures in which major cities had a patron deity responsible for the fate of the city and the surrounding territory, while the city itself would be personified as his consort.[6] The personification of Jerusalem allows prophetic texts to address the city as distinct from its inhabitants.

This figure, Lady Zion, can be identified more readily in Hebrew than in English text, because Hebrew distinguishes between masculine and feminine forms of both finite verbs and pronouns. Consequently, some of these Lady Zion texts may not be immediately clear to students reading only English Bibles, but critical commentaries should help explore the imagery when she appears. The extent of her role in prophetic texts can be noted by the fact that she appears in all four prophetic scrolls, though not equally dispersed across these collections. Lady Zion appears most prominently in Isaiah 40–66, where she appears in no fewer than seven passages (49:14–26; 51:17–52:10; 54:1–17; 57:6–13; 60:1–22; 62:1–12; 66:6–13). She appears regularly in Jeremiah in both judgment texts (chaps. 2–8) and restoration texts (chaps. 30–31). In Ezekiel, she appears prominently with Lady Samaria in two extended texts often labeled as porno-prophetic (chaps. 16 and 23). In the Book of the Twelve, the fate of Zion and Jerusalem as a place is a central concern in Joel and plays a significant role in other restoration texts (Amos 9:11–15; Obad. 17–21). That being said, the *personified* Lady Zion appears as a character for the first time in Micah 4:8–13, though she is named in Micah 1:16 and she speaks in 7:8–10. From this point forward, she appears periodically in at least three other passages (Zeph. 3:14–20; Zech. 2:7–10 [MT 2:11–14]; and 9:9–13; note also Nah. 1:15 [MT 2:1], where Judah is addressed in feminine singular). These texts treat Lady Zion in increasingly positive terms.

The figure of Lady Zion allows the portrayal of intimate relationships: she can be both wife and mother, and as a woman she can be addressed rhetorically in both positive and negative terms. Negatively, the rhetoric of prophetic texts tends to speak about her or address her as an unfaithful wife or a prostitute who seeks multiple lovers other than her husband. Drawing upon ancient Near Eastern cultural beliefs, the husband, YHWH, must therefore punish and humiliate her for her actions. Used positively, as in Isaiah 49–66 and the Book of the Twelve, she serves as YHWH's wife: their relationship has been restored, her children shall be returned and empowered, and she will be restored to her former position of royal power.

Hosea's Children

Finally, the inversion of literary images into images of hope and restoration can be readily seen at the beginning of the Book of the Twelve with the symbolic names given to the children of Gomer in Hosea 1–3. These three chapters represent three units: chapter 1 is a report, chapter 2 is a metaphorical exploration, and chapter 3 is an autobiographical account. In the first two chapters, the names of the children play a role as both signs of judgment and signs of hope.

Hosea 1 uses a biographical style to recount the birth of three children whose names symbolize YHWH's judgment of Israel: "Jezreel," meaning "God sows, scatters seed"; "Lo-ruhamah," meaning "not loved"; and Lo-ammi, meaning "not my people." The first of these names alludes to the place (Jezreel) where Israel's most powerful dynasty came to an end with the death of Ahab. At the end of Hosea 1, these messages of judgment are reversed into words of promise: the day of Jezreel becomes a day of gathering rather than scattering (1:11 [MT 2:2]), while the people will be called "loved" and "my people" (2:1 [MT 2:3]).

Hosea 2 compares YHWH as husband to Israel, who is an unfaithful wife who chases after lovers. Near the end of this metaphorical comparison, the names of the children reappear as words of promise. YHWH will respond to Jezreel and sow (zāraʿ) him in the land (2:22–23 [MT 2:24–25]); YHWH will love "Not-loved"; and he will call "Not-my people" by the name "My people" (2:23 [MT 2:25]).

Interpreting Reversals of Judgment

What one sees in prophetic promises and restoration texts should not really come as a surprise. Yet the significance of these restoration texts should not be overlooked. The quantity of restoration texts compared to judgment texts is rather small, but the cumulative effect of these hopeful passages, which appear in virtually every prophetic writing, makes an important theological claim: God has not abandoned the people of Judah and Israel, despite the experience of the destruction of Jerusalem and Samaria. These restoration texts renew the call for commitment and hope. They hope for the rebuilding of ruined cities and a renewal of the land's productivity. They also remind the people of the destruction of the kingdom and their abandonment of YHWH. Prophetic judgment texts challenge the behavior of the leaders (religious and political) as well as the people themselves.

These confrontations often claim direct links between human behavior and divine punishment of the entire nation. This direct cause-and-effect theology has been justly challenged by later theological paradigms (both Jewish and Christian). When viewed rhetorically, however, the prophetic writings serve a didactic function. They do not function merely as a vehicle for announcing YHWH's wrath. They are designed to recount prophetic messages to admonish those who will listen to act in ways consistent with the covenant obligations of YHWH's followers. At times, some passages leave the impression that nothing will survive YHWH's judgment. These same prophetic collections, however, correct themselves by acknowledging the importance of finding hope and seeking YHWH after the punishment happens. Both affirmations reflect the message of the prophetic collections.

These prophetic collections are set within the time frame of the eighth century BCE through the Persian-period writings. They portray YHWH's concern for YHWH's people, and they testify to the experience of the word of YHWH through YHWH's prophetic messengers (including those who compiled these writings). They call for justice, righteousness, and fidelity to the God who does not abandon them. They pronounce judgment and offer hope. The vacillation creates an uneasy tension but challenges modern readers to consider both aspects. Oppression leads to judgment, because YHWH stands on the side of the oppressed; but even in times of judgment YHWH stands ready to act for the welfare of those who choose to walk the paths of YHWH.

7

Developing a Hermeneutical Approach

The art of applying biblical texts to modern life, called hermeneutics, constitutes a far more complex task than can be explained in the space remaining. Nevertheless, consideration of two basic questions can launch one onto the path of one's own application process. These two guiding questions basically concern identity and procedure. In other words, they address the questions who and how.

FOR WHOM IS THE MODERN MESSAGE INTENDED?

Much of the interpretive process to this point has focused upon recognizing and understanding elements within and behind the text. The process has sought to articulate how the text would have been understood in its compositional context, a time and place far removed from our own experience. In so doing, one has isolated and contemplated elements from a very different cultural setting. Now, however, one should consider how the setting of the target audience might, or should, affect one's interpretation. Answers to these questions will vary dramatically from student to student and congregation to congregation. Hence, interpreting one's own target audience represents a very personal process. A few questions and observations may help to focus the issues.

What bearing might the identity of the congregation have on whom within this text the congregants will, or should, identify? Sometimes the interpreter may decide the identity of the congregation makes no difference, but one should at least consider whether things like the congregation's ethnic identity or socioeconomic status will affect its understanding of a given text.

117

For example, consider how members of the congregation might respond to texts from Amos and Micah that confront the wealthy in their society. Initial responses toward the prophetic message of those of means in the congregation might be hostile or suspicious. Do you as the interpreter wish to build upon their discomfort or assuage it in order to talk about justice in society?

On the other side of the ledger, persons struggling economically might initially be drawn to these speeches because they sense in Amos and Micah someone who gets it, who understands the subtle ways in which society benefits those with means. Does the interpreter build upon these feelings? Further, does it matter that Amos and Micah would have been considered fairly well-to-do in their society because, as landowners, they themselves would have been considered part of the upper class?

Other identity markers should be considered as well. Does one's country of origin or one's political persuasion change one's predisposition toward a particular set of characters in the prophetic text? How might one's gender or age affect the way one hears a particular text? Sometimes the answers to questions like these require the interpreter to anticipate reactions from the congregation that might facilitate or get in the way of the larger message. Sometimes the interpreter may want to use these different responses to frame the message of the prophetic text for today.

How does preparing a message for a Christian congregation change how this text will be heard and understood? Careful consideration of issues related to this question should not be underestimated, but neither should they paralyze the interpreter. On the one hand, most Christian congregants have a more difficult time understanding prophetic texts than narrative texts in the Hebrew Bible. Further, many Christians intuitively experience the portrayals of God in prophetic texts as too vindictive, too angry, or too wrathful. On the other hand, time and time again mainstream Christianity has reaffirmed its conviction that the Christian canon includes the Hebrew Bible. These affirmations should spur the interpreter to find ways to make prophetic texts, and other Old Testament texts, relevant to the lives of people with whom they will be speaking. Already, working through a given text should provide a means of reflection that will help the interpreter make connections to the lives of people today. Prophetic texts deal with big issues, issues with which every generation and every congregation should come to grips: What do justice and righteousness mean in our context? What does it mean to be faithful to God? How does one respond to economic deprivation or political oppression?

Before turning to some strategic questions for appropriating texts, one important assumption should be stated emphatically at this point. One should always remember that these identity questions relate to the *interpreter* every bit as much as they do to the congregation. If one is not reflective of one's own need to hear the message of the text, the interpreter of prophetic texts can easily come across as aloof or condescending. Since many prophetic texts assume a certain degree of confrontation between YHWH and the people, the interpreter should be careful not to sidestep his or her own role in the interpretive process. It can become all too easy to associate oneself with God when preaching or teaching the Word of God. Similarly, since Old Testament prophetic texts typically portray prophets as those who proclaim God's word, it can become quite easy for either the congregants or the interpreter to assume that role. Such projections can, of course, lead to very powerful interpretations, if and when the interpreter feels the need to confront the congregation. On the other hand, these projections, if not controlled, can lead to a sense of self-righteousness or self-importance that can get in the way of larger ministry goals. As a rule, interpreters should find ways to include themselves among those whom the text addresses.

HOW DOES ONE ADAPT AN OLD TESTAMENT PROPHETIC TEXT FOR A MODERN COMMUNITY OF FAITH?

Three strategic issues should be addressed by the interpreter as important components of appropriating a prophetic text for modern context: clarification of identity, direct application, and drawing analogies. First, with whom within this text does one ask the congregation to identify? Probably nothing will affect the application, or reappropriation, of a prophetic text for a congregation more than this question. Given the confrontational nature and the polemical rhetoric involving YHWH, the prophet, and the people, interpreters of prophetic texts will often be asking congregants, at least implicitly, to critique something they are doing or not doing. Prophetic texts often mediate scenarios wherein the prophet confronts the people or their political and religious leaders. Accordingly, it is hard to reflect such texts without establishing some level of confrontation within the modern setting.

Doing so, however, creates the potential for two different congregational responses that could dramatically reduce the effectiveness of the message. On the one hand, if one speaks about relationships between YHWH, the prophet, and the people in the biblical text and then asks the modern congregation to identify with the people, the interpreter has created a direct modern parallel that implicitly leaves the interpreter in the role of the prophet. The danger here lies in the response from the modern congregants, who may well be offended by what they perceive as an attack. This response may be created intentionally or unintentionally, but one needs to be aware of this dynamic.

Experience of the backlash is particularly prevalent among younger ministers who in their zeal to translate the passion of the prophetic text find themselves unexpectedly assailed by some members of the congregation. The ability to confront a group of people effectively concerning any issue requires a level of the group's trust in the interpreter, and that trust has to be earned.

On the other hand, if the interpreter becomes overly fearful of how someone in the congregation might respond, then one runs the danger of having the application become simply irrelevant. If one does not in some way draw significant parallels between God's word to the community of faith in the past and God's word for today, then the interpretation runs the danger of being perceived as nothing more than a history lesson. Members of the congregation can then look smugly at people from the past whom God needed to change.

Often this happens because the Christian interpreter arbitrarily distinguishes between pre-Christian communities of faith and the church. Such hermeneutical assumptions, however, rarely do justice to the actual claims of the text. At best, they treat the addressees of the text benignly, as representatives of human behavior unenlightened by the Christian message. More likely, they can convey a subtle supersessionist or anti-Semitic message that somehow Christian communities of faith do not need to reflect seriously upon issues of communal justice, righteousness, compassion, and ethics. Finding one's way between these two extremes requires care from the interpreter who is asked, in some way, to take up the mantle and the message of the prophet.

Direct application of theological concepts represents a second strategy for interpreters to consider. When one asks what it is that the prophet expects from the community of faith with whom he is speaking, one quickly realizes that these expectations remain valid in modern, Christian contexts as well. Most American Protestants expect ministers to challenge them to live ethical lives, but they become uncomfortable quickly if and when ministers start asking them to think collectively and communally about covenant obligations. Concepts like justice, righteousness, fidelity, violence, and idolatry should be part of the fabric of faith for believing communities as well as individual believers. Questions regarding the specific nature of how one adapts these concepts into modern settings will undoubtedly differ from congregation to congregation and may even create debate within individual congregations.

Consider two examples: prophetic proclamations against idolatry and prophetic calls for justice. Modern congregations likely find it easy, at first, to side with the prophets against the worship of idols. So long as one defines idolatry as the worship of physical representations of a deity, most church members would hardly give a second thought to whether or not their congregation practiced idolatry. If, however, idolatry is defined as giving allegiance to any-thing that takes precedence over God, then an uneasy sense of discomfort will soon replace any smug sense of superiority. Congregations, and groups within congregations, might bristle at the suggestion that one's own church building might have become a kind of idol, because keeping up appearances, or keeping pace with the building programs of other churches, can have become more important than the missions that congregations perform in the name of God.

It is also doubtful that any congregation would openly declare itself to be against justice. After all, the opposite of justice would be injustice, and very few congregations would want to be accused of being a home of injustice. Yet debate will soon arise when one tries to define justice as the *proper* action for the community of faith in any given situation. For example, is it enough for a congregation to contribute to a community food bank in order to help feed the poor? Or should they devote their resources, financial and human, to changing unjust systems that perpetuate or accentuate problems faced by the poor?

These two illustrations begin to demonstrate how quickly prophetic chal-lenges, most of which are expressed to groups, can quickly cause congrega-tions to wrestle with questions of identity and purpose. Leading congregations to evaluate their response to injustice or their rejection of idolatry can upend the status quo, and that change can frighten many in the congregation. It can, however, also embolden a church to engage the world more concretely than it has in the past.

As was already suggested, the application of prophetic texts frequently involves drawing some kind of analogy between the community of faith in the past and its modern counterpart. This analogy may involve drawing parallel connections or contrasts between the two groups. Sometimes, prophetic texts may challenge the entire community of faith. At other times, these texts may challenge the community as a whole on behalf of a group within the com-munity. For example, prophetic texts may challenge Israel, Judah, or both because they are challenging the behavior of the national community—or culture—more than they are challenging the community of faith, who may be represented by the group that is suffering in the prophetic text. In cases such as this, it may be quite appropriate to draw parallels between the relationship of the church to its culture.

At other times, prophetic texts focus upon the improper behavior of the believing community itself. These words of admonition need to be heard as well. When congregations lose their collective will to evaluate their role in society, as well as their role as a worshiping community, then they have ceased to learn to live prophetically as a community.

CONCLUSION

The application of prophetic texts by modern communities of faith can be a challenging endeavor. It can be fraught with risk, but it can also rejuvenate communities of faith to ask the big questions: What does it mean to be a covenant community in the world today? What does it mean to call for justice and righteousness in a culture where the ends frequently justify the means or where pushing the limits of legalities takes precedence over asking the question, "Is it right?" It is rarely easy to hear the challenges expressed in prophetic texts and to ask what those challenges mean for the community of faith today. Not to do so, however, runs an even greater risk: losing the ability to speak boldly to issues of importance for both the community of faith and the culture at large. Prophetic texts challenge complacency with a power and a passion that testifies to the dynamic power of God's presence in this world.

Notes

Chapter 1: Getting Started

1. For further examples from the oldest surviving "Dream Book," see *COS* 1:53–54.
2. See B. A. Levine, "The Deir 'Alla Plaster Inscriptions," in *COS* 2:140–45. The material within these inscriptions was recorded around 800 BCE, while those who assume the exodus story reflects the kernel of a historical event typically date the exodus to the thirteenth century BCE.
3. Dates appear in headings in 1:1–3; 3:16; 8:1; 20:1; 24:1; 26:1; 29:1, 17; 30:20; 31:1; 32:1, 17; 33:21; 40:1. Only 29:1, 17 and 32:1, 17 disrupt this chronological order.
4. James D. Nogalski, "One Book and Twelve Books: The Nature of the Redactional Word and the Implications of Cultic Source Material in the Book of the Twelve," in *Two Sides of a Coin: Juxtaposing Views on Interpreting the Book of the Twelve/Twelve Prophetic Books*, Analecta Gorgiana 201 (Piscataway, NJ: Gorgias Press, 2009), 12.

Chapter 2: Analyzing Literary Parameters and Rhetorical Flow

1. The confessions of Jeremiah represent first-person prophetic complaints, some of which contain divine responses. Texts generally associated with this term include Jer. 11:18–23; 12:1–6; 15:10–12, 15–21; 17:14–18; 18:18–23; 20:7–13, 14–18.
2. Most critical commentaries will address significant changes of speaker and addressee in a given passage, but individual commentators frequently assume the changes without explaining them. In the last decade, software that parses the grammatical elements of the Hebrew text has become more readily available, both in university computer labs and to individuals willing and able to invest in these programs. Bible Works and the Libronix library system offer two of the more popular system for PCs, while the Accordance program performs these functions for Macs. Web sites containing interlinear presentations of the Hebrew and English can be found on the Web by using a search engine. Those Web sites that provide grammatical data for the Hebrew, however, are more helpful than those that provide only word-by-word interlinear glosses.

3. Mark Edward Biddle, "The Figure of Lady Jerusalem: Identification, Deification and Personification of Cities in the Ancient Near East," in *The Biblical Canon in Comparative Perspective*, ed. B. Batto, W. Hallo, and L. Younger, Scripture in Context 4 (Lewiston, NY: Mellen Press, 1991), 173–94; Christl M. Maier, *Daughter Zion, Mother Zion: Gender, Space, and the Sacred in Ancient Israel* (Minneapolis: Fortress Press, 2008).

4. Detailed discussion of the broader techniques would require more space than allotted here, as well as a knowledge of Hebrew. Classifying this phenomenon often requires careful attention to Hebrew word order, and it is often neither possible nor desirable to replicate this word order when translating into English. For further discussion of the phenomenon, see Robert Alter, *The Art of Biblical Poetry* (New York: Basic Books, 1985), 3–61, and Adele Berlin, *The Dynamics of Biblical Parallelism*, rev. ed. (orig. 1985; Grand Rapids: Eerdmans, 2008). Berlin's work, in particular, is filled with examples of the wide variety of parallelism with both Hebrew and English.

Chapter 3: Selecting Key Words

1. William P. Brown, *Seeing the Psalms: A Theology of Metaphor* (Louisville, KY: Westminster John Knox Press, 2002), 4–7.

2. For an excellent introduction to Old Testament metaphors for God, see Rex Mason, *Old Testament Pictures of God*, Regent's Study Guides 2 (Macon, GA: Smyth & Helwys, 1993).

3. See Isa. 1:4; 5:19, 24; 10:17, 20; 12:6; 17:7; 29:19, 23; 30:11–12, 15; 31:1; 37:23; 40:25; 41:14, 16, 20; 43:3, 14–15; 45:11; 47:4; 48:17; 49:7; 54:5; 55:5; 60:9, 14.

4. Jeremiah, Hosea, and Habakkuk have two references each, while 2 Kings (19:22) and Zechariah (14:5) contain the only other examples in the Nebiim.

Chapter 5: Analyzing a Unit's Relationship to the Context

1. Walther Zimmerli, "Vom Prophetenwort zum Prophetenbuch," *Theologische Literaturzeitung* 104 (1979): 481–96.

2. Chart adapted from James D. Nogalski, *Hosea—Jonah*, SHBC (Macon, GA: Smyth & Helwys, 2011), 344.

Chapter 6: Common Themes in Prophetic Texts

1. Isa. 1:21; 57:3; Jer. 2:20; 3:1, 3, 6, 8–9; Ezek. 16:15–17, 26, 28, 30–31, 33–35, 41; 23:3, 5, 19, 30, 44; Hos. 1:2; 2:4–5; 3:3; 4:10–15; 5:3–4; 6:10; 9:1.

2. See the discussion in Ehud Ben Zvi, *A Historical-Critical Study of the Book of Zephaniah*, BZAW 198 (Berlin: de Gruyter, 1991), 298–306, and Adele Berlin, *Zephaniah*, AB 25 (New York: Doubleday, 1994), 81–82.

3. Jer. 1:13–15; 4:6; 6:1, 22; 10:22; 13:20; 15:12; 16:15; 23:8; 25:9, 26; 31:8; 46:6, 10, 20, 24; 47:2; 50:3, 9, 41; 51:48.

4. See James D. Nogalski, "Presumptions of Covenant in the Book of Joel," in *Covenant in the Persian Period: From Genesis to Chronicles*, ed. Richard J. Bautch and Gary N. Knoppers (Winona Lake, IN: Eisenbrauns, 2015).

5. Ezra 3 creates confusion by dating the beginning of the rebuilding of the temple foundation two years after the exiles returned to the land in the reign of Cyrus (Ezra 3:8) under the leadership of Zerubbabel, some sixteen years prior to the time indicated in Haggai. According to Ezra 4, the delay was caused by enemies among the surrounding nations (see Ezra 4:1–5). Haggai and Zechariah contain no indication of this earlier attempt.

6. Outside of Judah and Israel, the city is often portrayed as the consort of the patron deity. These traditions are adapted within the Judean context by reference to Lady Zion (some translations prefer the literal rendering "Daughter Zion"). For more complete discussion of these texts in their ancient Near Eastern background, see Christl Maier, *Daughter Zion, Mother Zion: Gender, Space, and the Sacred in Ancient Israel* (Minneapolis: Fortress Press, 2008); Mark Edward Biddle, "The Figure of Lady Jerusalem: Identification, Deification and Personification of Cities in the Ancient Near East," in *The Biblical Canon in Comparative Perspective*, ed. B. Batto, W. Hallo, and L. Younger, Scripture in Context 4 (Lewisburg, NY: Edwin Mellen, 1991), 179–94; John J. Schmitt, "The Motherhood of God and Zion as Mother," *Revue Biblique* 92 (1985): 557–69; Aloysius Fitzgerald, "The Mythological Background for the Presentation of Jerusalem as a Queen and False Worship as Adultery in the OT," *Catholic Biblical Quarterly* 34 (1972): 403–16.

Index of Scripture

CPSIA information can be obtained at www.ICGtesting.com
Printed in the USA
LVOW11s0712160915

454202LV00001B/1/P